POETRY AND POP-UPS
AN ART-ENHANCED APPROACH
TO WRITING POETRY

MARY LOMBARDO

A publication of Linworth Learning
Linworth Publishing, Inc.
Worthington, Ohio

Published by Linworth Publishing, Inc.
480 East Wilson Bridge Road, Suite L
Worthington, Ohio 43085

ISBN 1-58683-082-1

TABLE OF CONTENTS

OBJECTIVES AND STANDARDS

This book was written with the following objectives in mind:

OBJECTIVE: Correlate learning activities with the concepts contained in the standards for the English language as compiled by the National Council of Teachers of English (NCTE).

OUTCOME: The lessons and activities in *Poetry and Pop-Ups* correlate with concepts presented in the standards developed by the NCTE.

OBJECTIVE: Lead children to discover that poetry is pleasurable for listening, reading, and writing.

OUTCOME: Introducing children to poetry in an enjoyable way helps develop appreciation for the art.

OBJECTIVE: Provide the opportunity to learn and practice elements basic to good writing.

OUTCOME: The outlined lessons in this book provide the opportunity to practice elements that are basic to all good writing whether it be essays, novels, short stories, reports, or poetry.

OBJECTIVE: Familiarize students with several forms of poetry and provide opportunities to create poems following those forms.

OUTCOME: After completing this writing unit, the students will recognize ten different forms of poetry and will have written at least one poem of each type.

OBJECTIVE: Demonstrate to the students that reading and following directions are important.

OUTCOME: Making pop-ups is not complicated, but the directions must be followed step-by-step.

Correlation with National Council of Teachers of English Standards*

The National Council of Teachers of English has developed 12 standards citing how students should be helped to develop appropriate language skills. The exercises in *Poetry and Pop-Ups* provide students the opportunity to become familiar with the use of language structure and conventions in a creative way and help teachers incorporate NCTE standards into their curricula.

*The complete list of standards can be found at www.ncte.com.

HOW TO USE THIS BOOK

There once were some kids who wrote rhymes
At all sorts of extraordinary times.
They wrote while they ate.
They wrote early and late.
And then sold their rhymes for some dimes.

Maybe *Poetry and Pop-Ups* won't have your students quite this enthusiastic about writing poetry but it's a fun introduction to the art form because it's centered around another art form—making pop-ups! Pop-ups are enjoyable and amusing whether they are the surprise in a greeting card, a stand-alone piece of art, or, as your students will discover, an illustration for a poem.

Poetry and Pop-Ups addresses ten different forms of poetry going from very simple color poems to the more challenging limericks and haiku. Although the book focuses on writing various kinds of poetry, learning the correct forms is not the most important goal of writing poetry. Emphasis should be placed on expressing one's thoughts and feelings to one's self and others.

There are 13 different types of pop-ups presented in this book. Some are more challenging than others, but all are easy to construct if the directions are followed step-by-step as given.

Chapters One and Two are written to assist the teacher in starting a poetry and pop-up unit.

- Chapter One, "Creating Poetry," outlines lesson plans for teaching the basic elements of good writing. There are Teacher Tips, Teacher Scripts, Classroom Activities and correlating Student Worksheets to introduce and reinforce each lesson.

- Chapter Two, "Creating Pop-Ups," gives materials needed and helpful hints for creating pop-ups.

The next three chapters of the book contain teacher scripts for teaching the various poetry forms. The instructions are in an easy-to-read format so that you can choose to copy any of the lessons for individual children or reproduce them for use on an overhead projector for the entire class to read. The instructions for each type of poem are accompanied by examples of the form along with directions for making different pop-ups. Classroom Activities and Student Worksheets are included.

HOW TO USE THIS BOOK

- Chapter Three, "Simply for Fun," introduces very simple forms of poetry: color poems, person poems, acrostics, concrete or shape poems, and simple rhymes. Directions for a different type of pop-up accompany each poetry form.

- Chapter Four, "Hooray for Holidays," provides the opportunity to practice the poetry forms learned in the preceding chapter by suggesting holiday poems and pop-ups.

- Chapter Five, "The Shapes of Poetry," contains more challenging forms: the limerick, cinquain, haiku, diamante, and the narrative poem. Two new types of pop-ups are introduced in this chapter along with an idea for combining pop-ups to make a multi-page book.

TO BEGIN:

Follow the suggestions in "Getting Started" by setting up a class library and motivating your students to read and memorize poetry. Use the suggestions in the Appendix to choose poetry books for the class library. Then follow the lesson plans in Chapter One for teaching the basic elements of good writing.

MAKING POP-UPS:

Assemble the materials needed for creating pop-ups that are listed in Chapter Two and you are ready to begin your poetry and pop-ups adventure! You might want to make a few of the pop-ups and put them on display before starting the poetry unit as an example of what the class will be learning.

POETRY FOLDER:

Ask each student to keep a file of all the Student Worksheets from this unit to use as references for writing poetry and constructing pop-ups in the future.

GETTING STARTED

LAYING THE GROUNDWORK

Since poetry is such a shadowy, will-of-the-wisp art to try to explain, nothing can match reading poetry to get a sense of what it is and what it is not.

Your students are probably familiar with and enjoy some poets such as the ever popular Dr. Seuss and Shel Silverstein whose rhymes have amused children for many years. There are many other poets who appeal to young and old alike and some of these poets and works are listed in the Appendix.

Poetry should be read for the sheer enjoyment of the sound, rhythm, and concise language, but it has to be a personal thing. Because backgrounds, likes, and dislikes differ, the understanding of the poets words will differ also.

This is not to say that, if an author's intentions are known, those intentions should not be brought into the discussion of a poem. Far from it. Everyone's ideas of the meaning of the poet's words will enrich the discussion and the understanding of universal truths. In the same fashion, what we, as individuals, bring to the writing of a poem will vary.

Reading the poems of others will help your students enjoy the art form and become proficient writers of poetry. To help them understand better how to write poetry, it would be helpful to review the fundamentals of writing that are given in Chapter One and then have a literary treasure hunt through various poems for those elements.

The Treasure Hunt

Tell the students they are searching for literary treasures. As they read poems for the second or third time, see if they can find examples of alliteration, word repetition, words that appeal to the senses, similes, and metaphors, and keep score as to the number of each found. Becoming familiar with how others use these basic writing techniques will create a path students can follow when creating their own works.

GETTING STARTED

BEGINNING THE POETRY UNIT

- **Build a classroom library** with poetry books that students will enjoy. You will find a listing of some of these books in the Appendix. Perhaps you can schedule a time for students to read one or two poems from their favorite authors and explain why they like them. If you have favorite poems, share them with your class and talk about what it is that appeals to you in those poems. Ask students to suggest poems for you to read to the class. In addition, choose some that you wish the students to become familiar with.

- **Study the basic elements** of good writing in Chapter One and do the included exercises with the students. Work through the Student Worksheets together or assign them for homework.

- **Be positive** about your students' and your own poetry attempts. Make this unit an enjoyable experience for all involved.

- **Encourage students to memorize** some of their favorite poems. This is an activity that students often enjoy. Or, if you prefer, have the students read poetry aloud to the class.

- **Post a wall chart** entitled "The One Hundred Lines Club" with each student's name listed. Record lines of poetry students memorize and/or recite to the class. When students reach 100 lines, they become members of the club. A simple computer-generated certificate can be given to each student who successfully becomes a member. The certificate could even be written in verse. At the end of this book is a sample you can reproduce and use. Make as many copies as you need.

THE ONE HUNDRED LINES CLUB

Student Name	Number of Lines									Total
Sally Jones	5	8	6							
Bobbie LaRoy	4	10	3	9	8					
Joey Blue	6	4	10	12	8					
Brittney White	5	8	8	9	6					

GETTING STARTED

PRESENTING THE POETRY UNIT

You have several choices when deciding how to best present this unit.

1. You may wish to do all the work during class time, instructing the students on the poetry form, practicing the form as a class, and having each student complete the Student Worksheets as a class assignment.

2. For some of the poems, you may decide to use an overhead projector and have the entire class read and follow directions together.

3. The Student Worksheets can also be sent home for homework with a note to parents. Inform the parents that you are studying poetry and ask for their help with homework assignments. If they take advantage of it, writing poetry with their children is an opportunity for the families to enjoy some quality time together.

4. Because children usually enjoy showing off the work they have done, consider having a poetry reading after the unit is completed. Invite parents and other classes to listen to your students recite some of their best work. Perhaps your classroom could even be arranged to look like a coffeehouse and student table servers could serve lemonade or tea!

5. Ask your librarian for names of magazines that publish children's work and see if your students wish to submit any of their poems. Here's a chance to practice letter writing.

OUR POETRY READING

CHAPTER ONE
CREATING POETRY

INTRODUCTION

Whenever you teach any category of writing, it is recommended that you write along with your students. Applying yourself, just as you are asking them to do, shows that you value writing and that you struggle to use the right words and feelings just as they do.

Sharing your work with them is important too. It can be difficult to let others hear what you have written and to have your work critiqued. Teachers who exhibit their work and accept constructive suggestions before asking students to do so serve as models.

Before you and your class begin to write, you will want to review some basic elements that will make the writing experience more satisfying and meaningful. Explanations of these basics follow, along with some Classroom Activities and Student Worksheets.

- **GETTING IDEAS:** deciding what to write about.

- **CHOOSING THE BEST WORDS:** using the most specific words.

  Alliteration: repeating initial sounds in neighboring words or syllables.

  Word Repetition: using a word throughout a piece for a certain effect or rhythm.

  Using the Five Senses to Create Images: using words that appeal to the senses.

  Similes and Metaphors: A simile is a figure of speech that compares two unlike objects using the words like or as. A metaphor is a figure of speech that gives attributes of one object to another dissimilar object.

- **VOICE:** expressing ideas in a unique, personal way.

- **ORGANIZATION:** writing in logical order.

- **EDITING/REVISING:** revisiting the piece to make sure it is logical and fluent, and checking punctuation, spelling, grammar, and capitalization.

GETTING IDEAS

TEACHER TIPS:

 Ideas for writing are all around us. They come from what we do; what we see; friends and acquaintances; our travel, whether it's just to and from school or around the world; pets; or the food we like or dislike. In other words, ideas are like leaves from autumn trees. They drift around us and fall at our feet waiting to be picked up and used.

TEACHER SCRIPT:

 As we begin our exploration of how to create different types of poetry, the first thing we will investigate is how to get ideas for our poems.

CLASSROOM ACTIVITIES:

1. Discuss some of the books or poems that the students are reading and see if they can articulate what they consider to be the main idea.

   For example:
   The main idea of the *Star Wars* movies is good versus evil.
   "The Road Not Taken," a poem by Robert Frost, is about making life choices.

2. On chart paper or the board, make a list of your favorite foods. Show the list to the students and then go down the list remembering little anecdotes about each item.

   List example:
   Cornish game hens

   Anecdote:
   When I was a newly married, army wife, my husband's commanding officer came for dinner and I put the hens in the oven and forgot to turn on the oven. At serving time I found myself staring at four pink, glistening, raw game hens!

3. Ask your students to list, in their writing folders or notebooks, their favorite foods. Ask for volunteers to relate stories about one of the foods they listed.

GETTING IDEAS

CLASSROOM ACTIVITIES continued:

4. On the chalkboard write headings for future lists. Ask the students for ideas. Some headings might be:

- Places Where I've Been
- Sports I'd Like to be Good At
- I Wonder...
- What Makes Me Mad
- What Makes Me Happy
- Excuses for Not Doing My Chores
- Why I Love/Hate Homework
- Ways to Use Gum besides Chewing
- New Uses for an Old Baseball Cap
- Ways to Conserve Water
- Red (or any color) Foods
- Favorite Movies/TV Shows/Books/Games

5. Give the students time to choose list headings and write in their writing folders or notebooks as many ideas for each list as they can.

Sports I'd Like to be Good At:
1. Basketball
2. Tennis
3. Baseball
4. Hockey
5. Skiing

6. After the students have several lists compiled, have each of them choose one idea from a list and write a short story or essay using that idea. Before they begin writing, you could choose one of your ideas and model writing a short piece based on the idea. Talk about your thought processes as you write.

STUDENT POETRY WORKSHEET

NAME: _____   **TOPIC: Getting Ideas**

Ideas for writing are all around you and only need to be recognized to be used. Think about one day of your life. What did you do from morning to night? Whom did you see? What did you wear? What did you eat?

1. List everything you did on that day.

I had _____ for breakfast.

I wore _____

I had fun _____

I watched _____

_____

_____

_____

_____

_____

2. Choose one of your activities that made you smile or feel happy and write several sentences about it.

_____

_____

_____

_____

_____

3. Now choose another of your activities that created a different mood for you (serious, sad, mad, worried) and write another paragraph.

_____

_____

_____

_____

_____

CHOOSING THE BEST WORDS

Covered in this section are several ways to encourage students to use words that will make their writing come alive. Using these writing techniques will help your students stretch their imagination to choose the most specific words for the meaning they intend.

ALLITERATION

TEACHER TIPS:

Alliteration is repeating initial sounds in neighboring words or syllables. Many poets use words that begin with the same letter to create a certain sound or effect in their works. It's fun to use alliteration, but it's best not to over-use one letter sound, as it's easy to cross the line from a fine alliterative phrase to a tongue twister. Following are two tongue twisters that demonstrate what over-using alliteration sounds like. Have fun trying to say them as quickly as possible. Then ask the students if they know some other examples that they could share with the class. Next, read the example of an alliteration and have your students read passages from other poets to give them a sense of how to use alliteration to their best advantage.

TEACHER SCRIPT:

Sometimes it can be tricky to keep an alliteration from turning into a tongue twister. Here are two famous examples of alliteration that are tongue twisters.

Peter Piper picked a peck of pickled peppers.
If Peter Piper picked a peck of pickled peppers,
Then where's the peck of pickled peppers Peter Piper picked?
—Anonymous

Betty Botter bought some butter
But, she said, this butters bitter;
If I put it in my batter,
It will make my batter bitter,
But a bit of better butter
Will but make my batter better.
So she bought a bit of butter
Better than her bitter butter,
And she put it in her batter
And made her bitter batter better.
—Anonymous

ALLITERATION

TEACHER SCRIPT continued:

Here is one example of what a good use of alliteration sounds like.

I set out to sea today
On a simple sailing boat.
"I want to see the world," I said,
"If I can stay afloat!"

CLASSROOM ACTIVITIES:

1. Ask the class to write as many short tongue twisters as they can in ten minutes. **Examples:**

Sister Susie sews shirts for soldiers.
Cute Cathy cooks kumquat candies.
Mellow Melvin mails melons to Managua.

The students will have fun sharing their tongue twisters. You might want to use them as a reading exercise by posting them on a bulletin board or on the exit door.

2. Emphasize again the difference between tongue twisters and alliteration. Reread the example of alliteration above as well as the examples below. Ask the students to pick out the alliterative words in each poem.

BIRDS OF A FEATHER
Birds of a feather flock together
And so do pigs and swine,
Rats and mice will have their choice,
And so will I have mine.
—Anonymous

THE PROBLEM
Prudence P. Prewitt, a pretty young girl,
Had a terrible problem, her hair wouldn't curl!
She poufed and she permed, but not one made a dent
Till she fastened her ringlets with rubber cement.

Notice in line two of "Birds of a Feather" the "s" is used both at the end of pigs and then at the beginning of swine. In line three the sound of "s" not the letter, is used in mice and choice. These are other examples of how alliteration can be used.

ALLITERATION

CLASSROOM ACTIVITIES continued:

3. Write a class alphabet poem of alliteration. Beginning with the letter "a," assign one or two letters to each student in your class. Ask each of them to write a phrase using a few words starting with the assigned letters to create word pictures. Remind students to include words that begin with other letters so they don't write tongue twisters!

The phrases can be as few as two words or as many words as they like, as long as they still make sense!

Examples:
ants and aardvarks are annoying
(All words start with "a," but the beginning sounds differ.)

big cargo boats bursting with bananas

clever and cunning Siamese cats

cream filled doughnuts, sugar dusted delights

When you have one or more phrases for all alphabet letters, put them together to make a poem entitled "Alphabet Alliteration" and post it in the classroom.

STUDENT POETRY WORKSHEET

NAME: _____   **TOPIC: Alliteration**

1. Tongue twisters are sentences where almost every word begins with the same letter or sound. **Example:** Seashells settling on the sandy shore.

Now you try it.

Write two examples of tongue twisters. Try saying them as fast as you can.

_____

_____

_____

2. Alliterative phrases repeat the same letter sound just as in tongue twisters, but the sound is used in fewer words. **Example**: The girls giggled at the gangly circus clown.

Now you try it.

Write two examples of alliterative phrases—be careful not to make them tongue twisters!

_____

_____

_____

3. Write a paragraph on any topic using several examples of alliteration. Here are some words to get you started.

Nouns: caterpillar, car, clown
     leaves, laughter, lamb
     scarecrow, spider, spaceman

Adjectives: cute, crawly, clumsy, careful
     lovely, loud, lonely
     scary, scraggly, special

_____

_____

_____

_____

_____

_____

WORD REPETITION

TEACHER SCRIPT:

Many poets use the same word, phrase, or whole sentence throughout a poem to create a certain feeling or sound. Repetition can be the best way to express an overpowering emotion, emphasize a description, or produce a special rhythm to the poet's words. The following poem is an example of a fun way to use word repetition.

JEREMIAH OBADIAH

Jeremiah Obadiah, puff, puff, puffs,

When he gives his messages he snuffs, snuffs, snuffs,

When he goes to school by day he roars, roars, roars,

When he goes to bed at night he snores, snores, snores.

When he goes to Christmas treat he eats plum-duff,

Jeremiah Obadiah, puff, puff, puff.

—Anonymous

CLASSROOM ACTIVITIES:

1. Put the poem "Jeremiah Obadiah" on the board or on chart paper and ask the students to read it. Then ask them to read it without repeating the words at the end of lines 1, 2, 3, 4, and 6. Can they hear what a difference it makes in the sound and the rhythm?

2. Read the following examples to the students to show them the various ways that repetition can be used.

    a) Words can be repeated at the beginning of each line.

I saw a fishpond all on fire

I saw a house bow to a squire

I saw a parson twelve feet high

I saw a cottage near the sky

I saw a balloon made of lead

I saw a coffin drop down dead

I saw a sparrow run a race

I saw two horses making lace

I saw a girl just like a cat

I saw a kitten wear a hat

I saw a man who saw these too,

And says, though strange, they all are true.

—Anonymous

WORD REPETITION

CLASSROOM ACTIVITIES continued:

b) A phrase can be repeated many times to get a chant-like rhythm to the poem.

NAUGHTY BUD
Splattered mud on my Sunday clothes
Naughty Bud, Naughty Bud.
Sprayed me with the garden hose
Naughty Bud, Naughty Bud!
Shouted, Now I've made you clean!
Naughty Bud, Naughty Bud!
How can brothers be so mean?
Naughty Brother Bud.

c) A phrase can be repeated twice, once at the beginning and once at the end of the poem.

Sleep, baby, sleep!
Your father herds his sheep:
Your mother shakes the little tree
From which fall pretty dreams on thee:
Sleep, baby, sleep!
—Anonymous

3. After reading and discussing the above examples, ask the students to think of a word or phrase whose sound they like or that has some meaning for them. It could be the name of someone or something. It could be an exclamation. It could be an alliterative phrase. Or, it could be a question like "Why?"or a phrase like "I wonder why?".

Why does the moon shine only at night?

Why do birds like to sit on telephone wires?

4. Ask the students to share the phrases they chose and agree on one to use for a class poem. With the students, write several lines of poetry, repeating the chosen word or phrase two or more times. If the phrase is used to enhance a description or create a mood, it will be repeated a few times. If it is used to create a rhythm, it will probably be repeated many times. Remember, the poem does not have to rhyme.

STUDENT POETRY WORKSHEET

NAME: _____   **TOPIC: Word Repetition**

Repetition of words can be used in poetry to make a description more clear, to create a mood, or to establish a rhythm. It can be used at the beginning of each line, throughout the piece of writing, or once at the beginning of the piece and once at the end. Remember your poem does not have to rhyme.

Now you try it.

1. Repetition at the beginning of each line:
   Create a poem on the lines below by starting each line with the words "I am."

   I am _____

   I am _____

   I am _____

   I am _____

   I am _____ (Put your name here.)

2. Repetition using a phrase throughout the entire poem:

   Choose one of these phrases and use it in every other line of a poem.
   "A very happy day!"   **"A very gloomy day!"**

   Examples:
   I scored a goal in the soccer game   or   **I fell out of bed this morning.**
   A very happy day!   **A very gloomy day!**

   _____

   _____

   _____

   _____

   _____

   _____

   _____

   _____

   _____

USING THE FIVE SENSES TO CREATE IMAGES

TEACHER TIPS:

In order to use words in writing which show, not tell, about something, authors have to engage the senses by using words that describe what they hear, taste, touch, see, and smell, and how they feel. The following poem is a good example of using words to paint a picture. Read the poem and discuss with the class.

ST. PAUL'S STEEPLE

Upon Paul's steeple stands a tree,
As full of apples as may be;
The little boys of London town,
They run with hooks to pull them down;
And then they run from hedge to hedge
Until they come to London Bridge.

—Anonymous

TEACHER SCRIPT:

Can you see the word picture the poet drew? Can you picture the tree heavily laden with apples and the little boys pulling them down with their hooks? What color are the apples? What are the boys wearing? How big are the hooks?

Notice that even though the author concentrated on the sensation of sight and drew a picture for us, we get a feeling of excitement that the boys must be feeling. Suppose the author had said, "The boys pulled the apples from the tree and went around the hedges till they came to London Bridge." Does that sentence present a picture as vivid as the one from the poem? Is there any feeling of excitement? The careful selection of a few words makes all the difference in showing, not telling.

CLASSROOM ACTIVITIES:

1. Ask the students to share with the class one sensation that has impressed each of them. Was it something they tasted, smelled, felt, touched, heard, or saw? It might have been the silky feel of a little puppy dog, or the crunch of a juicy apple, or the smooth creaminess of a bite of cheesecake, or the tight knot of sadness at the death of a loved one. Encourage each student to find words that will help the other students experience the sensation.

USING THE FIVE SENSES TO CREATE IMAGES

CLASSROOM ACTIVITIES continued:

2. List, as a class, as many words as you can that evoke each of the five senses.

   Examples:

   Taste: salty, hot, sweet, sugary

   Touch: fuzzy, rough, sandpapery

   Sight: bright, dull, red, distant

   Hearing: whisper, booming, roar, crash, sigh

   Smell: chocolate, popcorn, perfume, firecrackers

3. Hold up a picture. Ask the students to list all the objects and people they see in the picture and then have them write descriptive words for each object and person. Share descriptions and discuss which words make the picture come alive in their minds.

4. Put an object in a bag. Ask a student to reach into the bag but not look at the object. Ask the student to give the class a description of the object using words that will help them picture it and guess what the object is. Repeat this with several different objects.

STUDENT POETRY WORKSHEET

NAME: _____

TOPIC: Using the Five Senses to Create Images

In order to use words in writing which show, not tell about, something, authors have to engage the readers senses. They use words that tell exactly what they **hear, taste, feel, see, and smell.**

Now you try it.

1. Write short sentences or phrases using words that will appeal to each one of the senses.

Hearing: _____

Taste: _____

Touch: _____

Sight: _____

Smell: _____

2. Just for fun, see if you can write one sentence packed with words that appeal to as many senses as you can. You will probably never do this in a poem you are writing.

Example:
The long green rubbery pickle, dripping garlicky vinegar all over my new pink sweater, made my eyes water and twisted my tongue into pucker knots of delicious coolness.

_____

_____

_____

_____

_____

_____

_____

SIMILES AND METAPHORS

TEACHER SCRIPT:

Because writing needs to make efficient use of words, using similes and metaphors allows us to pack a lot of punch with as few words as possible. For instance, if you compare a person with a scrub brush, we know that he is bristly, gruff, strong, does a lot of work—all that with just two words!

A simile is a figure of speech that compares two unlike objects using the words "like" or "as." For example: My love is like a red, red rose!

A metaphor is a figure of speech that gives attributes of one object to another dissimilar object. For example: The ship plowed through the waves.

Here's a poem that uses many similes.

A HAPPY MAN

A man who smiles and never frowns
Is like the funny circus clowns;
When he jokes and laughs and sings
He's like a kitten swatting strings;
But when the clown grows blue and sad,
He's like a summer day gone bad
With clouds and rain to spoil the fun
And no more jokes for anyone!

CLASSROOM ACTIVITIES:

1. After reading "A Happy Man," post the poem on chart paper or display on the overhead.

- Ask your students if they recognize which words make up the similes.

- Ask them if they see meaning in any of the similes.

- Do the comparisons make sense to them?

- Can they explain the similes?

SIMILES AND METAPHORS

CLASSROOM ACTIVITIES continued:

2. Ask the class to pick an object and, as a group, apply the senses to it in a metaphorical way. Let's say the class chooses a pencil.

- What does it look like? **Example:** a pointed dagger.
- How does it smell? **Example:** fresh sawdust.
- What would it taste like? **Example:** dry and dusty.
- What might it say to you? **Example:** Why are you just sitting there so idly?
- How does it make you feel? **Example:** I've got to get working.

Then write a sentence using the responses to the questions.

Example:
The bright yellow pointed dagger wafts its fresh sawdust smell as it growls at me for sitting idly and goads me into getting to work on my poem.

3. Ask the students to pick two unlike items and compare them by asking what is the same about them and answering their own questions. It's like making up riddles!

Here are a few examples:

Question: How is a head like a desk?
Answer: They're both crammed full of stuff.

Question: How is an old cinnamon roll like yesterday's news?
Answer: They're both stale.

Question: How is a shoe like a book?
Answer: They both take us places.

Question: How is a ruler like a quiz?
Answer: They are both used to measure things.

Question: How is a blackboard like a student?

Question: How is a backpack like a brain?

Question: How is a pencil like a finger?

Question: How is a teacher like a book?

STUDENT POETRY WORKSHEET

NAME: _____   TOPIC: Similes and
                                                          Metaphors

Often authors will compare one object to another to make a description more clear to the reader by using similes and metaphors.

A simile uses the word "like" or "as" in the description.
Simile example: His laugh is like an elephant's trumpet.

A metaphor names the object as another object.
Metaphor example: My friend is a brave lion.

Now you try it.

1. Write two sentences using similes by comparing two objects or persons using the words "like" or "as."

   1. _____
   2. _____

2. Now write two sentences using metaphors by naming persons or objects as something very different.

   1. _____
   2. _____

3. Look around you. Choose two objects and write riddles about why they are alike.

   Question: How is a _____ like a _____?
   Answer: They are both _____.

   Question: How is a _____ like a _____?
   Answer: They are both _____.

VOICE

TEACHER TIPS:

 As our reason for writing changes, our style of writing changes. If we are writing a business letter, we will be more formal; a friendly letter, more casual; and a research paper, very serious. Our voice, however, does not change. We write as our hearts dictate, true to how we want to express ourselves.

If, as a teacher, you do nothing more than teach your students to remain true to their own voices, their own uniquenesses, you will have helped them take the most important step toward effective and fulfilling writing.

TEACHER SCRIPT:

All persons in this world have a very unique way of expressing themselves. When we are talking to friends or family, we never give a thought to staying true to our own style or voice. But somehow, when words are being written, we feel we need to sound like someone else: someone more educated, someone smarter, or someone more experienced in writing. So our writing can get stilted and, as a result, boring. As you do your writing exercises try to stay true to your own voice.

CLASSROOM ACTIVITIES:

1. Listen to different kinds of music: country western, classical, or rap. Discuss the differences and similarities between them.

2. Look at paintings by different artists or cartoon strips by different illustrators and discuss their differences and likenesses.

3. Read selections from two very different authors the children enjoy and discuss what makes those authors' books fun to read.

   • How does the writing differ?

   • How is it similar?

   • How can they tell one author from the other?

VOICE

CLASSROOM ACTIVITIES continued:

4. Show the students a variety of greeting cards or gift wrapping paper. Discuss the differences and similarities. Discuss why each is appropriate for a specific occasion. Relate this exercise to the fact that we write differently for different occasions.

5. Show the students a picture from a magazine or the newspaper. Ask them to imagine they are writing to a friend, telling them about the picture.

- Discuss what words would best describe the picture.

- Make a list of the suggested words on the board and ask each of them to write a short description using the words each of them feels are best and any others that would make the image clear to others.

- Ask for volunteers to read their descriptions and compare the styles of writing, not judging, but emphasizing styles. Some children may prefer long flowing sentences; some may be more concise in their sentence structure. Although many of the same words were used, the writing will vary from child to child. Each person has his or her own voice.

STUDENT POETRY WORKSHEET

NAME: _____   **TOPIC: Voice**

Just as musicians or artists can be recognized for their own particular style, authors are recognized by their own special kind of writing called their voice. You have your own voice or style of writing that is yours alone.

Now you try it.

1. Write a short note to a friend telling him or her about a party you will be having and invite him or her to attend.

_____

_____

_____

_____

_____

2. Now write a short note telling someone that you would like him or her to return something he or she borrowed from you.

_____

_____

_____

_____

_____

3. Tell how the writing was different in the two pieces you wrote. What words showed the difference? What words showed that the letters were written by you?

_____

_____

_____

_____

_____

_____

_____

ORGANIZATION

TEACHER SCRIPT:

Writing that isn't logical is confusing to the reader. Directions given in the wrong order will surely end up with someone getting lost. Recipes that don't give step-by-step instructions may precipitate a meal being tossed in the garbage. Good organizational skills in stating thoughts and ideas are necessary for good writing to occur. Good writing always has a beginning, middle, and ending in an order that makes sense.

CLASSROOM ACTIVITIES:

1. Write a short four- or five- sentence story on the board with the sentences written in the wrong order and ask students to put them in an order that makes more sense.

Example: (Write these sentences out of order.)

I wanted to make a chocolate cake.
I took out the flour, milk, sugar and butter.
I looked for the chocolate but couldn't find any.
I had to go to the store and buy some.
After I mixed all the ingredients and baked the cake, I sneaked a little taste.
It was delicious.

2. Write the following words on a permanent wall chart for easy reference: **first, second, third, before, after, next, finally, then, when.** Discuss how important these words are in organizing a piece of writing. Look back at the mixed up sentences in the first exercise and, as a class, rewrite them using some of these words to see if they make the directions clearer.

3. Write these out-of-order directions on the board and ask a few students to follow them. The proper order is in parentheses.

Stand up. (4)
Write your name on the piece of paper. (3)
Sit down. (1)
Finally, walk over to my desk and give me the paper. (5)
Next, get a piece of paper out of your desk. (2)

Ask why they are hard to follow as written and ask how the directions should read. What words helped to put them in order? After the directions are corrected and in the right order, ask a few students to follow them to show how easy it is when directions are given in a logical way.

STUDENT POETRY WORKSHEET

NAME: _____   **TOPIC: Organization**

Writing in a logical and orderly way helps others make sense of what you write. It makes good sense to practice writing clearly so others will understand you.

Now you try it.

1. Here are some directions that are not in the correct order. Number the sentences so they make sense.

   ☐ Then, write a sentence telling why you like school.
   ☐ Next, take out your paper and pencil.
   ☐ Read your partner's sentence.
   ☐ Trade papers with your partner.
   ☐ First, choose a partner for this writing exercise.

2. List the words that helped you put the sentences in order.

   _____   _____   _____

   _____   _____   _____

3. Choose a simple task and write directions for performing it. Use some of these words to make the directions clear: **first, second, third, before, after, next, finally, then, when.**

   _____

   _____

   _____

   _____

   _____

   _____

   _____

   When you are finished writing your directions, ask someone else to follow them. Discuss what made the directions easy or hard to follow.

EDITING/REVISING

TEACHER TIPS:

The final step in any piece of writing is making sure that there are no misspellings or punctuation or grammatical errors and revising the wording so that it is fluent. Reading the work aloud is a good way to check for errors and to ensure that it does not contain awkward phrasing. As you and your students read poetry, you should point out that, in most poems, each line usually begins with a capital letter.

CLASSROOM ACTIVITIES:

1. Put sentences that contain grammatical and spelling errors on the board and ask the students to correct the errors. Using samples from original work of students is helpful.

2. Write lines of poetry on the board leaving out the capitals at the beginning of each line and all punctuation. Ask the students to correct the capitalization and to insert punctuation that makes sense.

3. Review using a dictionary and spell-check on the computer to check spelling and grammar. While spell-check is not always accurate, it is still a useful tool.

4. Write a series of short choppy sentences on the board and read them aloud with the students to make the sentences more fluid.

Example:

John is my friend.

He is in my class.

We play checkers at school.

We play chess at school.

We are on a team together.

We play soccer on the team.

John has three sisters.

I have three sisters.

STUDENT POETRY WORKSHEET

NAME:_____   **TOPIC: Editing/Revising**

It is easier to read something when there are no punctuation or spelling errors and when your words flow in a pleasing rhythm. Always look over anything you have written and correct any errors. Read it out loud to see if it flows smoothly.

Now you try it.

1. There are 12 mistakes in the following paragraph. Rewrite the sentences correctly.

> **Jeffrey peked into the celar he was sur he had heard someting someting scare in the blacknes at the botom of the stairs. He wised his mom and dad were home.**

_____

_____

_____

_____

_____

2. Rewrite the following sentences so they sound more pleasing to the ear. Add or delete any words you think will improve the writing.

> **My dog's name is Tiger. He has fleas. The fleas itch. He scratches the fleas all the time. He is very uncomfortable. He gets grouchy. I gave him a bath to get rid of the fleas. I also bought him a red flea collar. He is a happier dog now. I am happier too.**

_____

_____

_____

_____

_____

3. On the back of this paper, write a paragraph about any subject you like. When you are done writing, read it aloud to see if it flows smoothly and correct any spelling, grammar, and punctuation errors.

CHAPTER TWO

CREATING POP-UPS

INTRODUCTION/INSTRUCTIONS

TEACHER TIPS:

Although pop-ups may seem complicated to construct, most are simple when the directions are followed step-by-step. Pop-ups are well worth the care that goes into building them for there is a great feeling of satisfaction when that little figure pops up off the page to make a three-dimensional illustration or greeting card.

Because instructions for making pop-ups are given on the Student Worksheets, it is suggested that you share the general guidelines listed below before any pop-ups are attempted. The directions on the worksheets are written in step-by-step, easy-to-follow language and provide a good opportunity for students to practice the skills needed for reading and following directions.

MATERIALS NEEDED:

- scissors
- glue or glue sticks
- pen or pencil
- markers or crayons
- ruler
- watercolors—if a sturdy paper is used
- two pieces of paper that are the same size

Any color computer paper or lightweight drawing paper will do. Construction paper can be used for the cover sheet of the projects, but it is hard to crease sharply, so should not be used to make the pop-ups.

FOLDING THE PAPER:

To make a fold, lay the paper flat and make sure the edges of the paper are together so you will get a straight fold. Press hard over the folds a few times to get a sharp crease. To make pop-ups, you will always cut your paper on the fold.

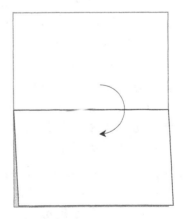

For a **hamburger fold**, fold the paper down, top to bottom, so the ends meet.

INSTRUCTIONS

FOLDING THE PAPER continued:

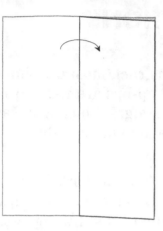

For a **hot dog fold**, fold it sideways, side to side, until the edges meet.

For a **book fold**, fold the paper hamburger style and then fold it again side to side so it looks like a little book.

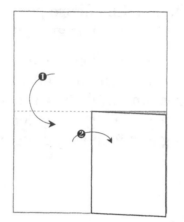

HELPFUL HINT:

To keep the paper from rippling when gluing two pieces of paper together, use as little glue as possible. Use tiny drops of glue whenever possible. Never put glue on the pop-up parts of the card.

TEACHER SCRIPT:

Pop-up cards are fun to receive because you never know what will jump out at you when you open the card. They're fun to give too because you can plan all kinds of surprises for your family and friends. You could make monsters, hearts, animals, or just some fancy words, that carry your message, pop up.

Poems are fun to put on greeting cards too. You can choose just the right words to fit the person who will get your card. Poems are just words strung together like beads on a bracelet. Just as jewelers know they have chosen just the right beads to fit together because of the way they look, you will know when you have chosen just the right words because of the way they sound.

Giving a friend or a family member a card you have made with a poem and pop-up that were created especially for him or her is a special way of saying "I care about you." It's like giving him or her a part of yourself. We are going to learn how to write many kinds of poems and make pop-up pictures to illustrate them. There are some poems and pop-ups that are very simple and there are some that are more challenging, but they're all a lot of fun to try.

CHAPTER THREE

SIMPLY FOR FUN

INTRODUCTION

TEACHER TIPS:

This chapter gives instructions for writing the simplest of all poems and is divided into four project sections. Each project presents examples of a type of poem, ideas for a Classroom Activity and a Student Worksheet on that type of poem along with Student Instructions for an accompanying pop-up art project.

Most of the poems are written in free verse, which is more like writing a story than writing a poem. Beginning with these easy poetry forms gives students a chance to apply the elements of writing that they practiced in Chapter One.

TEACHER SCRIPT:

The first poems and pop-ups we are going to learn are very easy and fun to create. You will be creating:

color poems—*poems about a favorite color;*
person poems—*about a friend or member of your family;*
acrostics—*using the letters of a word to make a vertical poem;*
concrete poems—*writing your poem around a shape;*
simple rhyming poems—*poems about anything you like.*

We will also learn how to make several different pop-ups: a talking animal pop-up, a person pop-up, a pop-up on a spring, and a mini-book pop-up.

PROJECT 1: COLOR POEMS

TEACHER SCRIPT:

The easiest poems to write are color poems, a form of free verse. Free verse just means that you can write whatever you like. You can write words or sentences and rhyme your words or not, but all of your words will be about one topic, in this case a color. The first poets who wrote free verse wanted their poetry to sound the way people talk naturally.

Color Poem Example:

BLUE

The endless sky above me,

Flowers bowing in the breeze,

My soft fuzzy mittens that keep me warm,

My baby sister's laughing eyes as she giggles at a tickle,

Blueberries in sweet-smelling muffins steamy hot from the oven,

And the silky, cool water of the lake where I swim in the summer's heat.

Blue, blue, blue, my beautiful blue!

PROJECT 1: COLOR POEMS

TEACHER SCRIPT continued:

How do you write a color poem? First, the author of the color poem we just read chose her favorite color. Then she thought about all the things that were that color and picked six of her favorite ones to write about. She wrote about the sky, flowers, mittens, her baby sister's eyes, blueberry muffins, and swimming in the lake.

Let's read the poem "Blue" one more time. How has the author tried to make you **see, smell, taste, feel,** *and* **hear** *the things she talks about in the poem? What words does she use to do that?*

Can you:
   see *the flowers bowing down in the breeze?*
   feel *the soft, fuzzy, warm mittens?*
   hear *the baby giggle when she is tickled?*
   smell *the sweet muffins and* **see** *the steam coming from them?*
   feel *the cool, silky water on your body?*

Those kinds of descriptions make the poem come alive for the reader.

TEACHER TIPS:

To get more familiar with color poems before you do the Classroom Activity or hand out the Student Worksheet, try reading *Hailstones and Halibut Bones* by Mary O'Neill. (New York: Doubleday, 1961.) This book is full of poems about color.

CLASSROOM ACTIVITIES:

• Choose a color and ask the students to help you think of objects that are that color.

• Make a list of those objects on the chalkboard.

• Now, think of descriptive words for those objects and make a list of those words.

• Use the objects and descriptions to write a class color poem.

STUDENT WORKSHEET PROJECT 1

NAME: _____   **TOPIC: Color Poems**

Color poems are really just a descriptive listing of things that are your favorite color.

Now you try it.

Fill in the following blanks to start.

My favorite color is _____

Here are some things that are my favorite color.

_____   _____

_____   _____

_____   _____

Now think:

Is there a special feel or sound or taste or smell that you associate with each item? Decide what words will describe those feelings best.

Write your color poem here using those descriptive words.

_____

_____

_____

_____

_____

_____

_____

PROJECT 1: PERSON POEMS

TEACHER SCRIPT:

Writing a color poem was pretty easy, wasn't it? Now, we are going to write a poem that is very much like a color poem but, because we're going to put our poem on a greeting card for a special person, we'll call our poem a person poem. Instead of writing all about a color, we'll write all about the person who is going to get the card. This is another poem that will be written in free verse just like the color poem.

Notice that these poems are written in sentences so it's just like writing a short story about a person.

Here are two examples of a person poem:

MY DAD

My dad's eyes are dark like Hershey's chocolate and they smile a lot.
My dad fixes things like pepperoni pizza with lots of stretchy, yellow cheese,
And the squeaky back door, and fights between me and my brother.
My dad's voice booms out over everybody else's at my soccer games.
My dad's arms are just long enough to give me a big, warm hug that makes me feel safe.
My dad loves me a lot and I love him too.

MY NEIGHBOR, MRS. SMITH

Some neighbors are good and some are bad
But my neighbor is the best!
On hot, sweaty days, I run through her sprinklers and she doesn't worry if I
accidentally run over a few flowers.
She doesn't get mad when my dog messes in her yard, though she does make me clean it up.
She makes great chocolate chip cookies and gives me some before I even ask!
What a great neighbor! Mrs. Smith, my friend.

CLASSROOM ACTIVITIES:
- Pick a character from a book that all the students are familiar with or a character from a movie they have all seen. Some suggestions: Cinderella, Harry Potter, Superman

- List some characteristics of the person you have chosen on the chalkboard.

- Write a person poem with the class using suggestions from the students.

STUDENT WORKSHEET PROJECT 1

NAME: _____   **TOPIC: Person Poems**

A person poem is just a listing of things about a certain person. Person poems are an example of free verse. They can be written in sentences or phrases.

Now you try it.

- First, decide who will get your card. His or her name will be the title of your poem.
- Make a list of all the nice things you can think of about that person.
- Describe him or her and, if you like, add how you feel when you are around him or her.

My Person Poem is for:_____

List of Qualities:

_____   _____

_____   _____

_____

Poem:

_____

_____

_____

_____

_____

_____

_____

_____

Read the poem out loud to yourself. If you need to add anything or subtract anything, do that now. Your person poem is complete and ready to be given to some lucky person! But not until you make a pop-up greeting card to go along with it.

PROJECT 1: TALKING ANIMAL POP-UPS

STUDENT INSTRUCTIONS
MATERIALS NEEDED:
- paper
- scissors
- glue
- ruler
- markers or crayons

POP-UP INSTRUCTIONS:

1. Fold one piece of paper in half hamburger style. Put a dot in the middle of the fold and cut a straight line about 1 or 1 ½" long, straight down from the dot.

2. Draw two more dots on the fold, each one inch away from the center dot. Connect each dot to the end of the one-inch cut you made in Step 1. You will have a triangle shape.

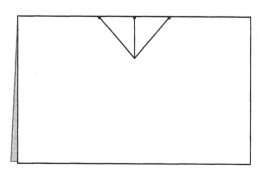

3. Fold along the triangle lines you have drawn, creasing sharply.

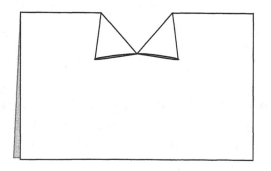

PROJECT 1: TALKING ANIMAL POP-UP

STUDENT INSTRUCTIONS continued

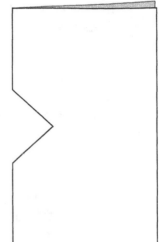

4. Unfold and open up the paper. You will see four triangles. Tuck the triangles inside the fold by creasing the lines you drew in the opposite direction they were creased previously. Crease the lines one at a time. This makes the pop-up. Close the paper, with the new folds facing inside and press down on it to flatten the creases. Turn the paper so the fold line is on the left, like a greeting card.

5. Take a second piece of paper and fold it hamburger style to use as the cover for your card. Glue the outside edges of the two papers together so that, when you open and close the card, the pop-up you made opens up.

6. Color the inside of the pop-up red. This is your animal's mouth.

7. Draw a picture of a frog or duck or any imaginary or real animal around the pop-up.

8. Write your poem around or on the side of the pop-up so it seems as if your animal is reciting the poem you have written.

You are my best friend——I like to play with you.
Please take me when you go to the beach and to the zoo.

9. Close the card and write the name of your poem on the cover. You might want to decorate the cover with pictures of things you wrote about in your poem.

PROJECT 2: ACROSTICS

TEACHER SCRIPT:

An acrostic is a poem that you read from top to bottom. It is sometimes a challenging poem to write because you have to think of words that start with the first letter you have written on each line.

To write an acrostic, you choose a name or other word and write it vertically on a piece of paper. Then you use the letter on each line as the beginning of words or sentences that you write about the subject.

(You can write these examples of acrostics on the board).

MOM
Marvelous storyteller,
Outstanding cook,
My mother.

SIS
Super
Intelligent
Sibling.

You can even write a phrase or a complete sentence for each line. Here is a poem that was written for a friend named LISA.

Long, dark hair and laughing, green eyes,
In a hurry, racing here and there.
She loves lilacs and lollipops
And I'm lucky that she likes me.

(Write this poem on the board, emphasizing the beginning letter in each line that forms the word LISA.)

CLASSROOM ACTIVITIES:

• Choose a word, from student suggestions, and write it vertically on the board, one letter on each line.

• Beginning each line with the letter written there, ask the students to suggest words and phrases that describe the word on the board.

• Read the poem when it is completed and see if there are any substitutions the students might suggest to make the description more vivid.

• If the acrostic is very short, you may want to write several acrostics, to give plenty of practice, before assigning the Student Worksheet.

STUDENT WORKSHEET PROJECT 2

NAME: _____   **TOPIC: Acrostics**

An acrostic poem is one that you read from top to bottom. You choose a word and put one letter of the word on each line. Then the lines of poetry must begin with that first letter.

Examples: HOME   JOE
              Home's a place   **J**umps for joy
              Of   **O**ver
              Much love and joy   **E**verything!
              Everything I need is there.

Now you try it.

Write two acrostics using one short word and one long word. For each poem, choose the name of a person or object and write vertically the letters of the name—one letter on each line. For each line, think of a word, a phrase, or a sentence that begins with the letter on that line and tells something about the person or object you chose.

ACROSTIC 1   ACROSTIC 2

_____   _____

_____   _____

_____   _____

_____   _____

_____   _____

_____   _____

_____   _____

PROJECT 2: PERSON POP-UP

STUDENT INSTRUCTIONS

MATERIALS NEEDED:
- paper
- glue
- marker or crayon

POP-UP INSTRUCTIONS:

1. Fold a piece of paper hot dog style. Open the paper, turn it over, and lay it on your desk so the fold points upward, like a tent. Flatten your paper and draw and color the person your poem is about so that half of the figure is on each side of the fold line.

2. Fold each side of the paper towards the middle fold line and crease sharply. This divides your paper into four long rectangles.

3. Take a second piece of paper and fold it hot dog style as well. This is the cover for your card. Write your poem on the outside of this piece of paper.

4. Open the cover and place your drawing on the inside of it. Match up the center folds making sure they go in opposite directions. Your picture should be showing.

5. Put glue along the back of the outside edges of the paper with your drawing on it. Glue your drawing to the inside of the card cover, about one half inch from each outside edge. Do not put any glue on the two middle rectangles where your picture is. When you open the card, your figure will pop out!

PROJECT 3: CONCRETE POEMS

TEACHER SCRIPT:

The poets who invented concrete poems wanted to say what they meant through pictures and images rather than just words. When we write concrete poems we use a picture of what we are writing about. We write the poem around a shape. For that reason, sometimes these poems are also called shape poems.

For instance a poem about love might be written around the shape of a heart, a cat poem around the shape of a cat, or a dog poem around the shape of a bone. The words do not have to rhyme. They can be a short story or some facts about the subject of the poem just like in our person poem. The poem itself can be as short or as long as you like. Here is a long poem which will need to be written on several lines around a shape.

THUMPER

Thumper's long, black hair is always shedding,

It gets into my mouth and over all my clothes!

He tracks big, muddy footprints on the floor and I have to clean it.

Sometimes he can be a nuisance!

BUT

When we play tug-of-war with an old, ripped towel

And fetch with a red rubber ball

And we curl up in bed, cozy warm under my patchwork quilt,

I know he's worth it!

And here's an example of a short concrete poem that will probably fit one time around a shape.

A home is a house with love for its walls.

CLASSROOM ACTIVITIES:

* Practice writing a shape poem together. Choose a subject and write a poem with the class.

* Draw an appropriate picture. Draw a second picture around the first and put a star on the larger one to show where you will begin to write the poem.

* Begin writing the poem on that line. If you do not have enough space, draw another figure around the two already drawn. Continue in this manner until the poem is written completely.

PROJECT 3: CONCRETE POEMS

Here is an example of a concrete poem written around a schoolhouse.

STUDENT WORKSHEET PROJECT 3

NAME: _____   **TOPIC: Concrete Poems**

A concrete poem is a poem that is written around a shape. A short poem will fit around one time while a longer poem may be written around the shape several times.

Now you try it.

Choose a subject for your poem. If you want to give a shape poem card to a friend or family member, think of something he or she likes or enjoys doing. Draw your picture and write your poem here.

PROJECT 3: SPRING-BACKED POP-UP

STUDENT INSTRUCTIONS

MATERIALS NEEDED:
- paper
- scissors
- crayons or watercolors
- glue

POP-UP INSTRUCTIONS:

1. Fold a piece of paper into a book fold. This will give you a piece of paper divided into four equal parts. Draw and color a picture on one of the parts making it as wide as you can. Cut the picture out and save the scraps.

2. Fold another piece of paper, of the same size, hamburger style. Place the paper on your desk with the fold on the top and write the name of your poem on the outside. This is your card.

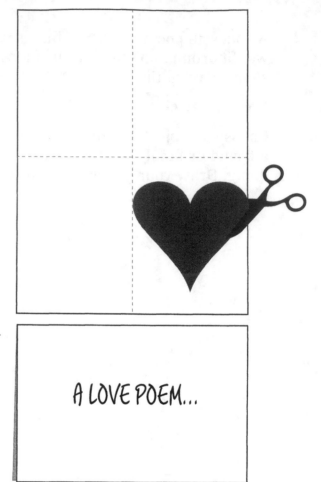

A LOVE POEM...

3. Open the card. Take the picture that you cut out and place it inside the card in the center of the bottom half, below the fold line. Trace around your picture. Then draw another identical line around the outside of the line you just traced. Allow at least a half inch between the two lines. Choose a spot somewhere on the outside line and draw a star there. This is were you will begin your poem.

STUDENT INSTRUCTIONS continued

4. Starting at the star, write the poem on the line so that you have to keep turning the paper to read the poem. If there is not enough room going once around the shape, draw as many lines as you need until the whole poem is written around your shape.

5. Cut two strips of paper about one inch wide and two inches long. Make springs for your picture by folding both strips of paper back and forth in opposite directions about five times. They will look like small fans. Crease the folds very hard.

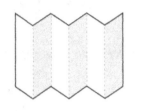

6. Glue one end of each spring to the back of the picture you cut out. One spring at the top and one at the bottom. Attach the cut out picture to the card by gluing the other ends of the springs to the shape you traced on the inside of the card. If your picture is a long one, like a bone or a fish, put your springs at either end rather than at the top and bottom. Close the card so that the title of your poem is showing. When the card is opened, the picture will pop out on its springs and your poem will be written all around it.

A LOVE POEM...

PROJECT 4: RHYMING POEMS

TEACHER SCRIPT:

Rhyming poems are fun because it can get really silly when you try to fit rhyming words together to make sense. Many poets you are familiar with, like Dr. Seuss and Shel Silverstein, write rhymes.

Here's a poem where two lines in a row rhyme.

I knew a girl whose name was Betty.
She really loved to eat spaghetti.
Morning, night, and every noon
She slurped it with a serving spoon.
She ate and ate and grew so round
Her feet could not move off the ground.
That was the end of my friend Betty
Who finally had enough spaghetti.

Here's a jump rope chant where every line rhymes.

As I was walking down the lake,
I met a little rattlesnake,
I gave him so much jelly-cake
It made his little belly ache.
One, two, three, out goes she!

—Anonymous

What is the rhyming pattern in this poem?

THE MAN IN THE MOON
The Man in the Moon, as he sails the sky,
Is a very remarkable skipper;
But he made a mistake when he tried to take
A drink of milk from the Dipper.
He dipped it into the Milky Way,
And slowly and carefully filled it;
The Big Bear growled and the Little Bear howled,
And scared him so that he spilled it!

—Anonymous

I'm sure you discovered that every other line rhymes, but did you notice something else the poet did? Listen to lines three and seven. There are rhymes within those two lines!

PROJECT 4: RHYMING POEMS

TEACHER SCRIPT continued:

What other rhymes can you remember? What is their rhyming pattern? An important thing to remember is that you should not get so wrapped up in trying to find rhyming words that you forget what you are trying to say in your poem. So, the first important thing to do is to pick a subject and decide what you want to say about it.

Then you can decide whether you want every line in your poem to rhyme, or every other line, or every two lines. It's your poem. You will write a list of rhyming words that are appropriate for your subject. Then you will fit other words around the rhyming words to tell a story. The story can be funny or serious and it can have as many lines as you like.

First, choose the subject. Let's say you decide to write a short nonsense rhyme about a cat and you want it to be as silly as can be. When you begin to write rhymes, short, silly ones are the easiest ones to write!

Next come the rhyming words. An easy way to find rhyming words is to choose the rhyme you want and then go through the alphabet to see how many words there are that end with that sound. Since we are writing a rhyme about a cat, that will be our main rhyme.

Some rhyming words would be: at, bat, cat, fat, hat, mat, Nat, pat, rat, sat, tat. Then we fit the rhyming words into a story about the subject.

THE KITTY CAT

There was an orange kitty cat
Who built a nest in dad's ten-gallon hat.
And lived there 'til she grew too fat.

That poem was kind of silly which is fun to start off with. But you can write a serious poem if you like. Here's a very short one.

Golden stars, as far as I can see,
Shining on my world and smiling on me.

PROJECT 4: RHYMING POEMS

CLASSROOM ACTIVITIES:

Write a rhyming poem with the class. You could start by using the "at" series of rhyming words—at, bat, cat, fat, hat, mat, Nat, pat, rat, sat, tat—and write a short poem similar to "The Kitty Cat" poem.

Next, try a longer poem with a different rhyming pattern. Make several lists of rhyming words. For instance, you might choose to write a poem about home-work and want to say what the class doesn't like about it. Select some words to rhyme that are related to the subject. Write them on the board.

Your words might be: **school, homework, play, study**.

Your rhymes might be:
school, cool, cruel, fool, pool, tool
homework, shirk, jerk, Kirk, lurk, perk
play, bay, day, hay, jay, lay, may, nay, pay, say, way
study, buddy, cruddy, fuddy-duddy, muddy

Here is an example of a Homework rhyming poem to get things going with your class. Next write one of your own. Try experimenting with different rhyming patterns.

HOMEWORK

Each day when I come home from school,

I think that life can be so cruel

Cause I'm always loaded with lots of study.

Now don't you think that's pretty cruddy?

Why should I work and waste my day

Instead of going out to play?

Whoever invented the first homework

Is, in my opinion, a great big jerk!

Next try writing a rhyming poem with the class about a mouse. Go through the alphabet and list the rhyming words that go with mouse—douse, grouse, house, louse.

Have the class choose another word to rhyme relating to the mouse theme and write those rhyming words on the board. Choose the rhyming pattern you want to use and write your poem.

STUDENT WORKSHEET PROJECT 4

NAME: _____   **TOPIC: Rhyming Poems**

The first two steps in writing a rhyming poem are to decide on a topic for your poem and then write a list of rhyming words that are suitable for your topic. *The Dictionary of Rhyming Words* can be a big help as you make your list. Another good place to find rhymes, as well as synonyms and definitions of words, is on the Internet at www.rhymezone.com

Now you try it.

Write your topic here. _____

Write your rhyming words here.

_____

_____

_____

_____

_____

_____

Now write your rhyming poem.

_____

_____

_____

_____

_____

_____

_____

_____

_____

PROJECT 4: MINI-BOOK POP-UP

STUDENT INSTRUCTIONS
MATERIALS NEEDED:
- paper
- scissors
- markers or crayons

POP-UP INSTRUCTIONS:

1. Fold a piece of paper twice so it looks like a little book. Write your poem on the outside cover.

2. Inside the book, draw a picture of one thing to show what your poem is about. Draw half of the picture on each side of the fold.

3. Open the paper and carefully cut out most of your picture. Leave the bottom of the picture attached on both sides of the fold.

4. Refold the book so your poem is again on the outside and the picture is inside. Crease the fold in the picture so it goes the opposite way of the book's fold. When you open the book, the picture will pop up.

CHAPTER FOUR

HOORAY FOR HOLIDAYS

INTRODUCTION

TEACHER TIPS:

Because no new poetry forms are introduced in this chapter, writing holiday poems provides a good opportunity to practice the forms learned in the previous chapter as well as the essentials of good writing introduced at the beginning of the poetry unit.

Holiday poems and pop-ups are perfect for greeting cards and the students may want to write several poems with accompanying cards and pop-ups for each holiday. If they are saving their Student Worksheets for poems and pop-ups, they can do much of their work at home on a voluntary basis or as assigned homework. Projects 5 through 8 are featured in this chapter and there are directions for seven new pop-ups.

TEACHER SCRIPT:

Now that you have learned and practiced some different kinds of pop-ups and poems, you can use any one of them to make holiday cards or books. There are also some new pop-ups suggested. Put your poem on the front of the card or inside, wherever you think it looks best.

We will be talking about several holidays but probably not all the holidays you and your family celebrate. After we're done learning about how to write poems and make pop-ups to illustrate them, it would be fun to make a list of all the holidays you celebrate and create poems and pop-ups for those special days.

PROJECT 5: NEW YEAR'S DAY

TEACHER SCRIPT:

On New Year's Day, we celebrate the beginning of a new year and say goodbye to the old one. In your New Year's Day poem you could write about some memories from the year gone by, tell what you are looking forward to in the new year, or tell someone you care about your wishes for them for the coming year.

You may want to write free verse repeating "I remember" at the beginning of some lines or an acrostic for the words "Happy New Year!"

I REMEMBER

I remember when we had the picnic last summer

And we played ball and ate crispy fried chicken as fat raindrops fell.

I remember how Grandma cried when I gave her the picture I found

Of her and Grandpa on the lake in a little gray rowboat.

I remember..........

PROJECT 5: NEW YEAR'S DAY

CLASSROOM ACTIVITIES:

Ask the students to share some of their memories of the previous year. Make a list of the shared memories on the board. Then, ask the class to help you create a class "I Remember" poem.

Then, write "Happy New Year" as an acrostic on the board and, as a class, complete it.

HAPPY NEW YEAR

Hats off to the old year
And make way for the new
Plenty of things to think about and
Plenty to do.
Yes!
N _____
E _____
W _____
Y _____
E _____
A _____
R _____

STUDENT WORKSHEET PROJECT 5

NAME: _____   **TOPIC: New Year's Poem**

You are going to practice two kinds of poems to welcome in the new year.

For an acrostic, you will write a word or phrase next to each letter below that begins with that letter. For your memory poem, simply fill in the blanks below with memories of the year that has just gone by. If you need more lines, just add them.

Now you try it.

H _____
A _____
P _____
P _____
Y _____
N _____
E _____
W _____
Y _____
E _____
A _____
R _____

I REMEMBER

I remember _____
I remember _____
I remember _____
I remember _____

PROJECT 5: NEW YEAR'S POP-UPS

STUDENT INSTRUCTIONS
MATERIALS NEEDED:
- paper for pop-up
- glue
- scissors
- construction paper
- stapler or needle and thread
- crayon or marker

POP-UP IDEA ONE:

1. Fold a piece of paper hamburger style. Turn the piece of paper so that the fold is on the left side. Open the paper, turn it over, and lay it on your desk so the fold points upward, like a tent. Flatten your paper and write "Happy New Year!" in big fancy letters diagonally across the paper.

2. Fold each side of the paper towards the middle fold line and crease sharply. This divides your paper into four equal rectangles.

3. Take a second piece of paper and fold it hamburger style as well. Turn the paper so that the fold is on the left side. This is the cover for your card. Decorate the cover to represent a Happy New Year's wish.

4. Open the cover and place the paper with your message inside. Match up the center folds making sure they go in opposite directions. "Happy New Year" should be showing.

5. Put glue along the back of the outside edges of the paper with "Happy New Year" on it. Glue your message to the inside of the card cover, about one half inch from each outside edge. Do not put any glue on the two middle rectangles. When you open the card, the letters will stand out to wish someone a Happy New Year!

PROJECT 5: NEW YEAR'S POP-UPS

POP-UP IDEA TWO:

1. Put two pieces of paper together and fold them in half three times. Draw half of a bell against the edge of the fold. Make sure your drawing is big enough to fill up most of the side of the paper. Then cut the bell out, cutting through all the layers of paper.

2. When you open up the cut out bell shape you will have eight bells folded in the middle. Crease the fold hard and either staple or sew all eight bells right down the middle on the crease.

3. Fold a piece of construction paper, or some other heavyweight paper, hamburger style to use as a cover for your card. Turn the paper so that the fold is on the left side. Place the folded bells inside the cover making sure the bell folds match the card fold.

4. Put small dabs of glue on the back of the bottom bell and glue it to the inside of the card aligning the fold in the bells with the fold line of the card. Next glue the two center bell halves together to hide the seam created by the staples or thread.

5. Take fourteen small pieces of paper, about one inch long and a half inch wide, and fold them back and forth in opposite directions a few times to create fan-like springs. Glue the springs between the bells at the bottom edges. When you open the card the bell will open up like an accordian.

This pop-up idea can be used for other holidays too. You can make pumpkins or hearts, Christmas trees or Christmas tree decorations or dreidels for Hanukkah.

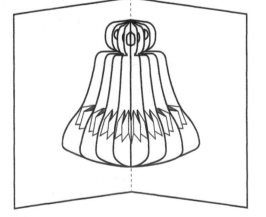

PROJECT 6: VALENTINE'S DAY

TEACHER SCRIPT:

Valentine's Day is our chance to tell people how much we care about them. A thoughtful way to do that is with a poem and a card you have made just for them.

Rhyming poems are ideal for Valentine's Day. A very well-known Valentine rhyme begins with:

   Roses are red. Violets are blue.
. . .and ends with whatever rhyme you want to put in.

You could say:
   You're my sweetheart, and I love you.

   Or

   I love you a lot. Do you love me too?

Can you think of some other rhymes for a special someone?

Another good poem to write for Valentine's Day (Mother's, Father's or Teacher's Day) is to write a person poem and simply list all the things you like about that person.

                              MY TEACHER
                     My teacher has a lot of patience.
                          He sits right beside me
            And explains things over and over till he's sure I understand.
                          And he makes work fun
         Like when we learned how to measure by seeing how far we could jump
                     And made lemonade in pints and quarts.
                     Even though the lemonade was kind of sour!

STUDENT WORKSHEET PROJECT 6

NAME:_____   **TOPIC: Valentine Poems**

You are going to write two different poems for Valentine's Day. Before you start writing, think of the people you would like to give cards to on that day.

You will be writing a person poem telling all the good things you can about the person who will be getting your poem. Then, you will write a short rhyming poem using the form below or choosing your own special form.

Now you try it.

Write your person poem here:

_____

_____

_____

_____

_____

_____

_____

_____

_____

_____

Write your rhyming poem here:

You can fill in the blanks below or write your own rhyming poem to the side of the form.

Roses are _____

Violets are _____

_____

_____

PROJECT 6: VALENTINE'S DAY POP-UPS

STUDENT INSTRUCTIONS

MATERIALS NEEDED:
- paper for pop-up
- glue
- scissors
- construction paper
- stapler or needle and thread
- crayon or marker

POP-UP IDEA ONE:

Here's a way to send a pop-up hug for Valentine's day or any other special day when you want to show someone you appreciate them.

1. Fold a piece of paper, five and half inches wide by eleven inches long, hamburger style. Along the fold, about one inch from both edges, cut a strip half inch wide about half way down the paper. These strips will be the arms for the hug. Leave two and a half inches in between the arms on the fold uncut.

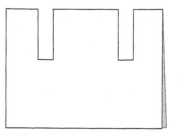

2. Open the folded paper. Pull the two strips toward you and refold them in the opposite direction. Close the paper and press hard to sharpen the creases so that when you open the paper the strips pop up.

3. Fold a second piece of paper, the same size, hamburger style to use as the cover for your card. Put glue on the back of the outside edges of the paper with the cut out strips. Make sure you do not put any glue where the strips are. Glue this sheet to the inside of the card cover.

4. Open the card and draw a hand on top of each strip near the fold. These are your arms. Draw a person around the two arms. When you open the card you will be giving someone a hug.

PROJECT 6: VALENTINE'S DAY POP-UPS

POP-UP IDEA TWO:

1. Fold a piece of paper hamburger style and then fold it again so it's like a little book.

2. Draw and color a large heart on the inside of the book so that half of the heart is on each side of the fold.

3. Lay the paper out flat, then refold it hot dog style so half of the heart is showing on either side. Cut out the top half of the heart, and then the bottom half, leaving a place on either side where it is still attached to the card.

4. Refold the card hamburger style again so the heart is on the inside of the book and pull the heart gently out from the card. Fold the center of the heart in the opposite direction of the card's fold so it will pop up when you open the card.

PROJECT 6: VALENTINE'S DAY POP-UPS

POP-UP IDEA THREE:
You can make a heart just like the bell we made for New Year's Day.

1. Put two pieces of paper together and fold them in half three times. Draw half of a heart against the edge of the fold. Make sure your drawing is big enough to fill up most of the side of the paper. Then cut the heart out, cutting through all the layers of paper.

2. When you open up the cut out heart shape you will have eight hearts folded in the middle. Crease the fold hard and either staple or sew all eight hearts right down the middle on the crease.

3. Fold a piece of construction paper, or some other heavyweight paper, hamburger style to use as a cover for your card. Turn the paper so that the fold is on the left side. Place the folded hearts inside the cover making sure the heart folds match the card fold.

4. Put small dabs of glue on the back of the bottom heart and glue it to the inside of the card aligning the fold in the hearts with the fold line of the card. Next glue the two center heart halves together to hide the seam created by the staples or thread.

5. Take fourteen small pieces of paper, about one inch long and a half inch wide, and fold them back and forth in opposite directions a few times to create fan-like springs. Glue the springs between the hearts at the widest part of the shape. When you open the card the hearts will open up like an accordion.

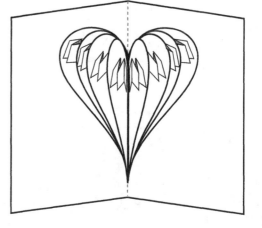

PROJECT 7: FOURTH OF JULY

TEACHER SCRIPT:

More than two hundred years ago, British colonists living in the new world fought Great Britain for their independence. When they were victorious, they named their country the United States of America.

On the Fourth of July we celebrate the freedom we enjoy as citizens of the country they founded. Our celebrations often include parades and picnics and displays of fireworks, bright and shining in the night sky.

We are going to write some poems for this very special day. Your Fourth of July poem could be about how happy you are to be an American. You could write a story poem about the many brave men and women who struggled to make us free.

Perhaps you will want to write about someone you know who is a firefighter or a police officer or a soldier who works today to protect our freedom.

You could write a shape poem around a flag or a cutout of our nation.

For example:

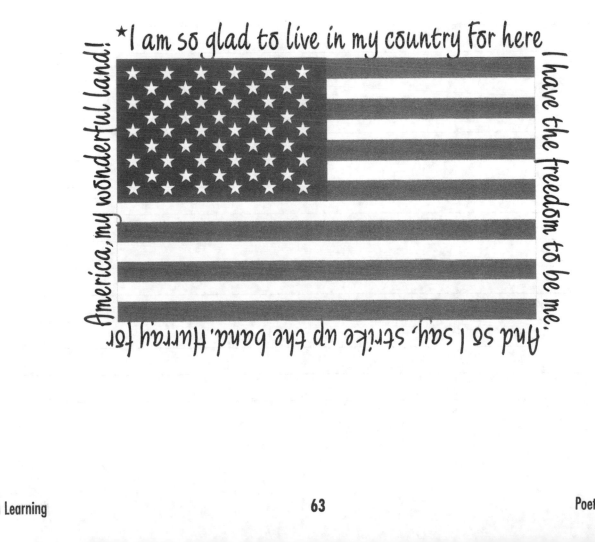

I am so glad to live in my country For here I have the freedom to be me. And so I say, strike up the band, Hurray for America, my wonderful land!

STUDENT WORKSHEET PROJECT 7

NAME: _____   **TOPIC: Fourth of July**
                                                                              Poem

Fourth of July is a very special holiday for all citizens of the United States. On that day we celebrate the birth of our nation.

For our Fourth of July poem you are going to write a rhyming poem using words that remind us of our great country, the United States of America. Some of the words you may want to use are listed here with some rhyming words to get you started. Finish going through the alphabet to find more rhymes for each word. Add any other words you want to use in your poem.

free: be, country, glee, he, she, key, liberty _____

brave: cave, gave _____

land: and, band _____

pride: bide, bride, chide, died _____

Now you try it.

_____

_____

_____

_____

_____

_____

_____

_____

_____

_____

_____

_____

_____

_____

PROJECT 7: FOURTH OF JULY POP-UPS

STUDENT INSTRUCTIONS

MATERIALS NEEDED:
- paper
- glue
- scissors
- red crepe paper
- crayon or marker

POP-UP INSTRUCTIONS:

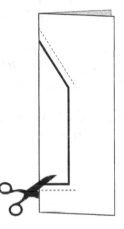

1. Fold a piece of paper hot dog style. On one side of the paper draw half of a rocket four or five inches long on the folded edge.

2. Keeping the paper folded, cut out the top half and the bottom half of the rocket leaving it attached to the paper in the center.

3. Open the paper and push the rocket toward you. The rocket's fold should be in the opposite direction of the paper's fold so that the rocket pops out when the paper is opened. Color the rocket.

4. Cut out about four or five thin strips of red crepe paper, no longer than three inches each, and glue them to the uncolored side of the rocket so it looks as if they are streaming from the tail end.

5. Fold a paper hot dog style to use as the outside of the card. On the outside of the card write "Happy Fourth of July" or "Happy Independence Day." You can write your poem here too. Glue the two papers together. Do not put glue on the pop-up rocket part.

6. Open the card and draw stars and pictures of firework explosions to complete your Fourth of July card.

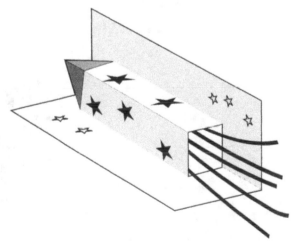

PROJECT 8: FALL HOLIDAYS

TEACHER SCRIPT:

Since ancient times people have held celebrations when they finished harvesting the crops and were looking forward to the beginning of winter. Halloween is one of our present-day celebrations that evolved from those times so very long ago.

Thanksgiving Day is a newer holiday that celebrates the end of harvesting. It originated with the Pilgrims almost four hundred years ago. They wanted to give thanks that they had had a good harvest and had found friends to help them survive in the New World.

We are going to write some poems and make some pop-ups to celebrate our fall holidays. If you like, you can use your poems and pop-ups for cards to give to others to wish them a happy holiday.

(Note: This would be a good time to review the voyages and settlements of the first American settlers.)

STUDENT WORKSHEET PROJECT 8

NAME: _____

TOPIC: Fall Holidays
Poems

A good poem for fall holidays would be an acrostic. Think of all the things you are thankful for that match the letters in the word "Thanksgiving" and all the spooky things you can think of for the letters in "Halloween." Here are a few lines to get you started.

Headless horsemen in the night
Autumn winds howling and screeching
Lost spirits searching for a home
L _____
O _____
W _____
E _____
E _____
N _____

Thanks for
Home
And
Nice friends
Kittens and puppies
S _____
G _____
I _____
V _____
I _____
N _____
G _____

PROJECT 8: FALL HOLIDAYS POP-UPS

STUDENT INSTRUCTIONS
MATERIALS NEEDED:
- paper
- glue
- scissors
- crayon or marker

POP-UP IDEA ONE:

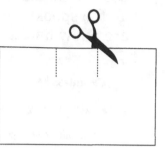

For either fall holiday, you can make a pop-up of a table with something sitting on it. For Halloween it might be a jack-o-lantern or it might be a plain pumpkin or a cornucopia for Thanksgiving.

1. Fold a piece of paper hamburger style. In the middle of the fold, cut two lines about two inches deep and two inches apart. This is the table. Open the folded paper. Pull the table strip toward you and refold it in the opposite direction. The table's fold will be in the opposite direction of the center fold. Close the paper and press hard to sharpen the creases so that when you open the paper the table pops up.

2. Draw, color and cut out a jack-o-lantern with a tab on its bottom on another sheet of paper. Make sure it will fit on your table. Do not color the tab. Fold the tab up toward the uncolored side of the jack-o-lantern and glue the bottom side of the tab to the top of the table near the edge of the table's fold.

3. Use a paper spring behind the jack-o-lantern to help it sit up straight. Cut a strip of paper as wide and long as you need and fold it back and forth in opposite directions a few times to create a fan-like spring. Glue one end of the spring to the back side of the jack-o-lantern and the other end to the paper behind it.

4. Fold a second piece of paper hamburger style to use as the cover for your card. Glue the cover to the back of the paper with the pop-up table. Do not put glue behind the table cutout. Line up the center fold of the cover with the center fold of the inside sheet. The folds should be going in the same direction. You can write your greeting or a poem on the outside cover of your card.

PROJECT 8: FALL HOLIDAYS POP-UPS

STUDENT INSTRUCTIONS continued
POP-UP IDEA TWO:
Here is a way to make people pop-ups.

1. First make a table as you did for your jack-o-lantern. Then draw different Halloween or Thanksgiving characters no taller than three inches. You could make a scarecrow, a witch, a ghost, a Pilgrim, a Native American, or any character you want.

2. Color the front of your character and then glue it to the front of the table so it looks as if your figure is standing.

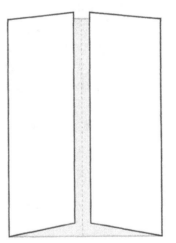

POP-UP IDEA THREE:
Here's another way to make people pop-ups.

1. Fold a piece of paper hamburger style then open it and lay it flat. Fold each side of the paper towards the middle fold line and crease sharply. This divides your paper into four equal rectangles. You will have three folds and four long rectangles.

2. Keeping the paper folded, turn the paper so that the two middle rectangles are facing you on top and the two outer rectangles are folded underneath. Draw a picture of a Pilgrim man in one rectangle and a Pilgrim woman in the other holding hands. Their outside hands should go to the outer edges of each rectangle.

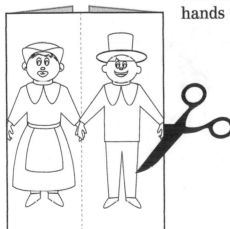

3. Leaving the paper folded, cut the Pilgrims out. **Leave the center hands connected.** The outer hands should be on the fold lines.

STUDENT INSTRUCTIONS continued

4. You should have four attached Pilgrims. Two women and two men holding hands. Color them. Fold another piece of paper hamburger style. Turn it so the fold is on the left hand side. This will be the cover for your card. Open the cover sheet and lay the four attached Pilgrims across the center fold, colored side up.

5. Put glue on the backs of the two outer Pilgrims and glue them to the inside of the cover. One outer Pilgrim should go on one side of the inner cover and the other outer Pilgrim should go on the other side of the inner cover. The middle two Pilgrims should be laying across the center fold. Do not put any glue on the middle two Pilgrims. Make sure the fold between the middle two Pilgrims goes the opposite way of the cover fold when you close the card. When you open the card the two middle Pilgrims will pop out.

CHAPTER FIVE

THE SHAPES OF POETRY

INTRODUCTION

In this chapter we cover five poetry forms that are more challenging than those previously taught. They are not, however, too difficult for you and your students to master and they are a lot of fun to write. Projects 9 through 13 are featured in this chapter and there are directions for two more pop-ups.

Before any writing is done, it is helpful to read aloud several poems of the form being studied to acquaint the students with the rhythm and format of the poetry, making it easier for them to imitate those aspects of each poem.

PROJECT 9: LIMERICKS

TEACHER TIPS:

Limericks are fun to write, but they can be challenging too. Before beginning to instruct the students about limericks, you will want to read some limericks to them so they get the feel of the rhythm and flow of the form. "The Hopeful Trout and Other Limericks" (Boston: Houghton Mifflin Co., 1989) by John Ciardi has some amusing limericks that the students will enjoy.

After you have read some poems and discussed the limerick form, write the two limericks given in this section on the board or on chart paper. Do not put the stress marks in until you have explained their meaning. Then, as the students listen to syllables that are stressed, they can help put the stress marks in the correct places.

TEACHER SCRIPT:

Now that we are familiar with how limericks sound we are going to be trying our hand at writing them. You can write limericks by starting the way you did for simple rhyming poems. You will make lists of rhyming words. You will need two different sets of rhymes.

Unlike free verse, limericks have a certain rhythm and they always have five lines. The first, second, and fifth lines rhyme with each other and the third and fourth rhyme with each other.

Another thing to watch in a limerick is that there are certain words that are said louder or harder than the other words. Lines 1, 2, and 5 have three words or syllables that are said harder and lines 3 and 4 have two words or syllables that are said a little harder. When we say some words or syllables harder than others we call that stressing the syllables. Stressed syllables are kind of like a beat note in music. We mark stressed syllables with a mark like an apostrophe.

PROJECT 9: LIMERICKS

TEACHER SCRIPT continued:
Listen to this limerick and see if you can hear which words or parts of words sound louder than others.

> There once' was a ti'ger named Sam'
> As meek' and as sweet' as a lamb.'
> But he got' in a rage'
> And escaped' from his cage'
> He came back' when they offered him ham.'

Let's read it together and see if we can put the stress marks where they belong.

Now let's read this limerick to see if you can guess which words are said a little stronger than the others. Which are the stressed syllables?

> There once' was a per'son named An'na
> Who start'ed to eat' a bana'na.
> She threw' down the peel'
> Right un'der her heel'
> And slid' all the way' to Savan'nah.

CLASSROOM ACTIVITY:

Write a limerick with the class. The story you tell can be as silly as you like, but it does have to be about the same person or thing.

Try to get the rhythm right, but if your lines don't exactly match the rhythm, don't worry. Enjoy the process and keep practicing. Limericks take a lot of practice.

Ask for suggestions for the limericks. The following pattern can be followed. The blanks indicate the number of syllables still needed on each line.

> There once was a _____ _____ named _____ _____
> Who wanted to _____ _____ and _____ _____.
> He _____ _____ and _____
> And _____ _____ _____ _____
> Then finally _____ _____ _____ _____ _____.

STUDENT WORKSHEET PROJECT 9

NAME: _____   **TOPIC: Limericks**

Limericks have a certain rhythm and they always have five lines.
The first, second, and fifth lines rhyme with each other. The third and
fourth lines rhyme with each other.

Now you try it.
- Decide on a person or thing as the subject of your limerick.
- List two different sets of rhyming words that have something to do with
  your subject.

Rhyming Words:

Set one: _____

Set two:_____

- Then, for your first limerick, try filling in the blanks in this framework.
  The blank lines tell you how many syllables to put in.
  (For instance, the word lion would take up two of the blank lines.)

There once was a _____ named_____ _____.

Who wanted to _____ _____ _____ _____ _____.

He _____ _____ _____ _____

Then _____ _____ _____ _____

And ended up _____ _____ _____ _____ _____.

On the back of this paper, write as many limericks as you want using the
framework above. You may want to write one about an animal at the zoo
or circus because the pop-up you will learn to make shows an animal in a
cage.

PROJECT 9: ANIMAL-IN-A-CAGE POP-UP

STUDENT INSTRUCTIONS
MATERIALS NEEDED:
- paper
- glue
- scissors
- crayon or marker

POP-UP INSTRUCTIONS

1. Fold a piece of paper hamburger style. Find the middle of the fold, cut two lines on either side of the middle about two inches deep and three and a half inches apart. These lines are the sides of the cage. If you want black bars for your cage, color the inside of this small section that you have cut out.

2. Measure and cut an odd number of same-sized strips between your first two cuts.

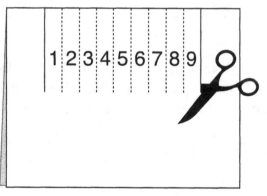

3. Beginning with the second strip on either end, cut out every other strip. If you end up with nine sections, you will cut numbers 2, 4, 6, and 8. This leaves the bars of the cage.

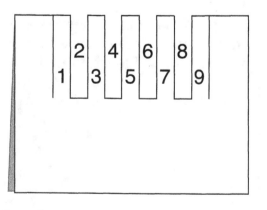

STUDENT INSTRUCTIONS continued

4. Open the paper. Pull the cage strips towards you and refold them in the opposite direction. The bars of the cage will be folded in the opposite direction of the center fold. Close the paper and crease hard. When you open the paper the bars of the cage will pop out.

5. Choose an animal for your cage to draw and color. Cut out your animal adding a tab to the bottom of it. Fold the tab towards the back of your animal. Make sure your animal will fit in your cage.

6. Fold another piece of paper hamburger style to use as the cover for your card. Glue the cover to the back of the paper with the cage. Make sure the center folds match up and are going in the same direction. The folds on the bars of the cage will still be going in the opposite direction. Do not put any glue behind the bars of the cage.

7. Place your animal in the cage. Glue the bottom of the tab on the animal to the inside bottom of the cage. Your animal should look as if it is standing or sitting inside the cage. If your animal needs help standing up straight, use a paper spring to anchor it to the back of the cage. You can make a spring by cutting a small rectangle piece of paper that will fit on the back of your animal. Fold it back and forth in opposite directions a few times to create a fan-like spring. Glue one end of the spring to the back of your animal and the other end to the back of the cage. When you open the card you will see an animal-in-a-cage pop-up.

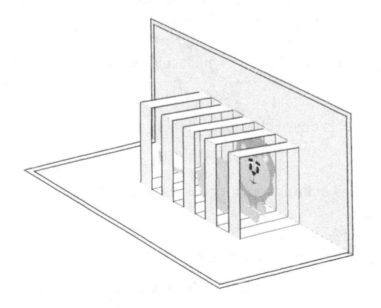

PROJECT 10: THE CINQUAIN

TEACHER TIPS:

You will want to write the examples of the cinquain (sin kane) on the board or on chart paper so the children can read along with you and see the pattern they will be following. The pattern is very simple: two syllables in the first line, four in the second, six in the third, eight in the fourth, and back to two for the last line in the poem.

This is a good poem to write when you want to sneak in some review about subjects, adjectives, nouns, and verbs. The first line is the subject of the poem; the second line is made up of adjectives describing the subject; the third line has verbs ending in "ing"; the fourth line goes back to nouns which express feelings; and the final line renames or tells something about the subject of the poem.

TEACHER SCRIPT:

A cinquain is a poem which always has five lines. Each line has to have certain kinds of words and the words have to have a certain number of parts or syllables. Sounds complicated? It really isn't once you get the idea.

CLASSROOM ACTIVITIES:

Write the following on the board, both the explanations and the sample poem to explain and show what a cinquain poem is.

Line 1 has two syllables (word parts) which tell the subject of the poem

Snowflakes

Line 2 has four syllables describing the subject.

Wet, white, lacy

Line 3 has six syllables action words (verbs ending in "ing")

Falling, drifting, sticking

Line 4 has eight syllables about feelings

Happiness, wonder, delight, glee

Line 5 has two syllables giving another name for the word in line 1.

Jewels

PROJECT 10: THE CINQUAIN

CLASSROOM ACTIVITIES continued:

Next, write this example of a cinquain on the board as a reminder to count by twos. Two for the subject, four for describing, six for some action, eight tells about feelings, then back to two for another name!

Cinquain Example:

```
              1  2
            Summer,
          1    2    3 4
        hot, fun, lazy,
       1   2   3 4      5 6
      swimming, biking, playing,
     1 2 3   4 5     6 7     8
    Excited, happy, thankful, glad.
        1        2
      No School.
```

Now write a cinquain about winter with the class. Take suggestions from the students, but here are some ideas in case you get stuck.

Winter
Cold, snowy, wet
Skiing, sledding, skating
Excited, energized, active,
Fun Times!

STUDENT WORKSHEET PROJECT 10

NAME:_____   **TOPIC: The Cinquain**

Remember to write a cinquain you have to count by twos! 2, 4, 6, 8, 2
- **Two syllables** in the first line
- **Four syllables** in the second line
- **Six syllables** in the third line
- **Eight syllables** in the fourth line
- **Two syllables** for the last line

Now you try it.

Pick a subject: **(2 syllables)**

_____

Describe it: **(4 syllables)**

_____

Give some "ing" action words: **(6 syllables)**

_____

Tell how it makes you feel: **(8 syllables)**

_____

Think of another name for the same thing: **(2 syllables)**

_____

That's your cinquain!

Remember, try to keep to the pattern, but if you can't, just do your best to say what you want to say. Write another cinquain on the back for more practice.

PROJECT 10: A CINQUAIN POP-UP

STUDENT INSTRUCTIONS

MATERIALS NEEDED:
- paper
- glue
- scissors

Here's an easy pop-up to go with any cinquain you write. It is a pop-up that can be many things. You just have to use your imagination.

POP-UP INSTRUCTIONS:

1. Fold a piece of paper hamburger style. Turn the piece of paper so that the fold is on the left side or keep the fold on the top. This will be your card. Cut out a rectangular strip of paper, any size that you want as long as it fits inside the card. Fold the strip of paper back and forth several times creasing it hard, creating a fan-like spring.

2. Attach the spring to the inside of your card. Glue one end of the spring to one side of the card and the other end of the spring to other side of the card. The spring will cross over the center fold. When you open the card the spring will pop out and can be used as a part of many things.

Here are some suggestions for using the spring as the pop out part of a picture. Remember: the spring should cross over the center fold of your card.

- Use a spring for steps for a school or a house.
- Draw a picture of a ballerina and use the spring as her tutu.
- If you draw a picture of a musician, the spring can be an accordion.
- The spring can be a fan too.

What other ways can you think of to use the spring?

PROJECT 11: HAIKU

TEACHER TIPS:

We usually think of a haiku (hie koo) poem as being a very rigid form with five lines and following a syllable pattern of five, seven, five. Actually, the most important facet of haiku poetry is that it shares a moment in time with another person, whether it follows the pattern or not.

While it is good to know what the pattern is and to try to follow it, capturing a thought or scene and expressing it in the best and most vivid way possible should be the goal for your students.

It is helpful to read examples of haiku poems to the students before they begin to write so they can get a feel for what a haiku is like. A good book for this purpose is "Red Dragonfly on My Shoulder." It contains 13 haiku poems translated from the Japanese by Sylvia Cassedy and Kunihiro Suetake. (USA: HarperCollins Publishers, 1992)

Write the haiku poems that follow on the board or on chart paper. Before beginning instruction, point out that the lines do not, as in other forms of poetry, begin with a capital letter.

TEACHER SCRIPT:

The poetry form called haiku comes from Japan and is meant to capture a moment in time and create images so others can share that moment with the author. Many times a haiku poem is about some part of nature.

A Japanese poet named Matsuo Munefusa who lived from 1644 to 1694 was a master of the haiku form. He is very famous under the name Basho. An interesting story is how he got his nickname. When he wanted to find some quiet place to write his poetry, Basho would go to a hut made of plaintain leaves. These huts were called basho-an. So people started calling him Basho.

Here is a haiku written by Basho that has been translated from Japanese.

> on a barren branch
>
> a raven is seen perching
>
> in the autumn dusk

What moment in time has Basho captured and how does he create an image for us to share that moment with him? He chose a specific kind of bird on a bare branch just as evening falls in the autumn of the year. He used very few words to create a clear picture in our minds. Would it be hard or easy to draw a picture of the moment Basho shares with us in his poem?

PROJECT 11: HAIKU

TEACHER TIP:

If you have time for the students to actually draw pictures of what is described in this poem, they will better appreciate how the right choice of words can paint a vivid picture.

TEACHER SCRIPT:

Usually, the haiku has only three lines that do not rhyme. The first line of the haiku has five parts or syllables, the second line has seven syllables, and the third line has five syllables. The lines do not begin with a capital letter. Here's an example:

```
1  2   3    4   5
frothy ocean waves
1   2  3 4  5  6   7
thunder on sandy shore, then
1   2   3   4  5
whisper out to sea
```

When first beginning to write haiku poems, it is best not to worry about the number of syllables. It is better to capture a moment in time exactly as you wish to share it with others. Concentrate on writing words that make it easy for your reader to draw a picture of what you are describing.

Here's another haiku. Does it have the right number of syllables on each line? Count them and see. Does it draw a picture in your mind?

```
snowflakes fall gently
painting red roofs and bare trees
with frozen silence
```

The important thing to remember about writing a haiku is that you are like a photographer. You have a picture in your mind of a memory and you use words to make others see your picture.

TEACHER TIP:

It is very difficult to write a group haiku because every one has different memories. If you have a memory you would like to share, perhaps you could walk through the steps of writing it as a haiku to demonstrate the process to the students.

STUDENT WORKSHEET PROJECT 11

NAME: _____   **TOPIC: Haiku**

A haiku tries to capture a moment in time so it can be shared with others. It uses very few words so each word you use is important in creating a picture for someone else to see.

Remember there are three lines in a haiku. The lines do not begin with a capital letter and the syllable pattern is 5-7-5.

Now you try it.
Pick a moment that you remember vividly, a moment that you would like to share with someone. Don't worry about the pattern as you write your memory. Do try to paint a clear picture with as few words as possible.

_____

_____

_____

_____

_____

_____

_____

_____

_____

When you have your memory written, look at the pattern of a haiku and see if you can fit your words into that pattern.

_____ _____ _____ _____ _____
5 syllables

_____ _____ _____ _____ _____ _____
7 syllables

_____ _____ _____ _____ _____
5 syllables

PROJECT 12: DIAMANTE

TEACHER TIPS:

Here is another poem that is useful for reviewing parts of speech. Students usually enjoy writing the diamante because it is written in a diamond shape and because of the clever way it changes subjects midway through the poem.

The diamante has seven lines and each line contains certain parts of speech.

The first three and one-half lines refer to one subject and the second three and one-half lines refer to another subject that is somehow associated with the first one. For instance, the poem you will be using as an example is about a dog and its master. Any two subjects may be used for a diamante as long as they are somehow associated with each other.

The pattern for a diamante is as follows:

Line 1 is a noun, one of the subjects.

Line 2 has two adjectives describing the noun.

Line 3 has three verbs with an "ing" ending describing the subject.

Line 4 has four nouns (two about the first subject and two about a second subject that comes in line 7).

Line 5 has three verbs ending in "ing" describing the subject in line 7.

Line 6 has two adjectives describing the subject in line 7.

Line 7 is one noun, the second person or thing the poem is about.

TEACHER SCRIPT:

A diamante poem has seven lines and is shaped like a diamond. It is an easy poem to write because the pattern tells exactly what kind of words you need to write on each line.

The diamante is a fun poem to write because the first half is about one person or thing and the second half is about another person or thing.

PROJECT 12: DIAMANTE

TEACHER SCRIPT continued:

In the poem I'm going to read to you, the first half describes a dog and the second half, beginning in the middle of line 4, describes the dog's master.

> *Line 1 is a noun, one of the subjects. (dog)*
> *Line 2 has two adjectives describing the noun. (playful, obedient)*
> *Line 3 has three verbs with an "ing" ending describing the subject.*
>   *(running, jumping, fetching)*
> *Line 4 has four nouns, two about the first subject and two about the second*
>   *subject that comes in line 7. (friend, companion, trainer, caregiver)*
> *Line 5 has three verbs ending in "ing" describing the subject in line 7.*
>   *(feeding, brushing, teaching)*
> *Line 6 has two adjectives describing the subject in line 7. (loving, strict)*
> *Line 7 is one noun, the second person or thing the poem is about. (Master)*

Dog

Playful, obedient

Running, jumping, fetching

Friend, companion, trainer, caregiver

Feeding, brushing, teaching

Loving, strict

Master

You can write a diamante poem about the sun and moon, day and night, rose and thorn, bow and arrow, skates and skateboard, soccer and basketball, school and home, or any other pair of words that go together. Other possible topics are mother and child, happiness and sorrow, sky and earth, and apples and oranges.

CLASSROOM ACTIVITY:

Take suggestions for topics from the students and write a diamante as a class project.

Write the format on the board so that you can follow it as you write.

1   noun (the first subject)
2   adjectives
3   "ing" verbs
4   nouns (two about the first subject and two about the second subject)
3   "ing" verbs
2   adjectives
1   noun (the second subject)

STUDENT WORKSHEET PROJECT 12

NAME: _____   **TOPIC: Diamante**

Follow the pattern below for your first diamante. The words we will use for this diamante are moon and sun.

- Write moon on the **first line**.

- On the **second line**, choose then write two adjectives that describe the moon. (big, shiny, round, changeable, distant, mysterious)

- On the **third line**, choose and write three verbs that end in "ing."
  These words will tell what the moon does.
  (circling, lighting, gleaming, growing, orbiting, waiting)

- On the **fourth line**, write two nouns that tell about the moon and two nouns that tell about the sun.
  (moon: satellite, orb, ball, crescent)
  (sun: star, universe center, light, life)

- On the **fifth line**, write three verbs that end in "ing" telling about the sun.
  (shining, heating, lighting, blazing, comforting, burning)

- On the **sixth line** write two adjectives that tell about the sun.
  (hot, fiery, gaseous, radiant, bright)

- On the **seventh line**, write the word sun.

Line 1 _____

Line 2 _____

Line 3 _____

Line 4 _____

Line 5 _____

Line 6 _____

Line 7 _____

Now you try it.

On the back of this paper write your own diamante. Then look back over the pop-ups you have learned and choose one that best suits your poem.

PROJECT 13: THE NARRATIVE POEM

TEACHER TIPS:

You may have already read some narrative poems to your class and discussed what constitutes a narrative poem. Narrative poems, although usually long, are of no particular length and they deal with dramatic situations where a main character has a problematic situation which he or she resolves by the end of the poem. Many famous narrative poems relate to love or war or both.

The narrative poem was born from the time that telling stories to groups was a form of entertainment and it was the forerunner of all poetry.

TEACHER SCRIPT:

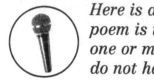

Here is a poem for you to try called a narrative poem. The narrative poem is usually the simplest form of poetry. Basically, it is a story about one or more characters who have a problem they must solve. The poems do not have to be any special length and they can rhyme or not.

Writing a narrative poem is just like writing a story. The poem must have a beginning, a middle section, and an ending. It must be about at least one person who has a problem that is solved by the end of the poem.

Some very famous poems like "The Song of Hiawatha" or "The Midnight Ride of Paul Revere" are examples of narrative poems.

In "The Song of Hiawatha" the main character, Hiawatha, first must build a sturdy boat and gets help from his forest friends to do this. Then, he goes hunting for a huge fish, the sturgeon, and, after slaying the sturgeon, is rescued by more of his friends.

In "The Midnight Ride of Paul Revere" the main character, Paul Revere, must ride to let the colonists know whether the British are coming by land or by sea.

Writing a narrative poem is just like writing a story.

    1. You decide on a main character.

    2. You invent a problem.

    3. You find a solution to the problem.

You might even want to write a true story about yourself and a problem you solved.

PROJECT 13: THE NARRATIVE POEM

TEACHER TIPS:

Read the following poem to your students and then ask them to name the characters, the problem, and the solution.

GOOD FRIENDS

Tom and Brent, good friends were they,
Until an unhappy fateful day
When, fearful of failing a history test,
Brent suggested that they ditch school.
"If you're my friend," he said,
"You'll go with me and not to school."
Tom hesitated and in that slow moment
Brent guessed that Tom would not agree.
"Are you my friend or not?" he cried. "Yes," stammered Tom. "I am your friend.
But, I have to go to school.
I have to, don't you see?" "No," shouted Brent. "I do not see."
"Friends stick together."
And he turned to run off:
But before he could,
Tom grabbed him by the arm and said,
"Come on, let's walk and talk.
I'll teach you all I know. Don't worry.
You'll pass the test. I'll help you all I can.
Friends help each other and I'll help you."
So off to school they walked
Discussing the Revolutionary War,
The colonies, and England's king.
"Thanks," said Brent when the day was done
The test taken and passed.
"It was nothing," Tom said, with a big half-circle smile.
"It's just friends being true
You're for me, I'm for you."

TEACHER SCRIPT:

Who are the characters? (Tom and Brent)
What is the problem? (Brent wants Tom to ditch school because he thinks he will fail a history test.)
What is the solution? (Tom wants to go to school but he wants to stay friends with Brent. He tells Brent he won't ditch school, but he will help him to pass the history test.)

STUDENT WORKSHEET PROJECT 13

NAME: _____   **TOPIC: The Narrative**
                                                                        Poem

Remember, narrative poems are stories about problems and how the problems are solved. They should have a beginning, a middle, and an end. Your narrative poem can be about something that really happened to you or you can make up a story.

Now you try it.

Choose a character or two.
Characters:_____

Invent a problem for one or both of them.
Problem:_____

_____

Think of a way to solve the problem.
Solution:_____

_____

Write the story out in poem form, beginning each line with a capital letter and using the best words you can.

_____

_____

_____

_____

_____

_____

_____

_____

_____

_____

PROJECT 13: BOOK POP-UP

STUDENT INSTRUCTIONS

MATERIALS NEEDED:
- paper
- glue
- scissors
- crayons or markers

Because you will have several pages to your narrative poem, you will need to make several pop-ups. Here is a way to build a long book that will hold all your pop-ups.

1. Choose pop-ups that you have learned to make that will go with the theme of your narrative poem. Make each pop-up separately.

2. Make each pop-up the same size. Glue a piece of paper to the back of each pop-up. Write the section of your poem on the inside of the pop-up that illustrates it.

3. Then, using as little glue as possible, attach the back of the first pop-up to the front of the second and continue in this manner until all your pop-ups are attached. This is your pop-up book.

What pop-ups will you choose to make to illustrate your narrative poem? That depends on the subject, the problem, and the solution.

For example:
In the poem about Tom and Brent, the first pop-up might be of two people; the talking mouth with either Tom or Brent drawn around it for parts when each of them talk; the rocket for when they discuss the Revolutionary War.

APPENDIX: POETRY CHILDREN WILL ENJOY

Here is listing of some books of poems that your students will enjoy. Some of the poets will be very familiar to them; hopefully some will become new and pleasurable acquaintances.

There are several books listed here that will be useful to you when you are helping students write specific forms of poetry. For instance, before writing color poems you might want to read *Hailstones and Halibut Bones* by Mary O'Neill. (New York: Doubleday, 1961.) Writing narrative poems could be preceded by the reading of some of Longfellow's narrative poems from *The Childrens Own Longfellow* (Boston: Houghton Mifflin Company, 1908.) Some of Edgar Allan Poe's poems serve as excellent examples of the use of repetition.

COLLECTIONS

Children's Counting Out by Gloria T. Delamar. North Carolina: McFarland, 1983.

The Children's Own Longfellow by Henry W. Longfellow. Boston: Houghton Mifflin Company, 1908. (Here are narrative poems: "The Song of Hiawatha," "Paul Revere's Ride," "The Building of the Ship".)

A Child's Treasury Of Poems edited by Mark Daniel. New York: Dial Books for Young Readers, 1986.

The Haiku Anthology edited by Cor VandenHeuvel. New York: W. W. Norton and Company, 1999.

Hailstones and Halibut Bones by Mary O'Neill. New York: Doubleday, 1961. (This book is filled with poems about color. It's a perfect book to read when the students are starting to write color poems in Project 1, Chapter Three.)

Hand in Hand, American History Through Poetry edited by Bennett Hopkins. New York: Simon and Schuster, 1994.

Heartsongs by Mattie Stepanek. Virginia: VSP Books, 2001. (This is a collection of poems written by an 11 year old boy.)

The Hopeful Trout and Other Limericks by John Ciardi. Boston: Houghton Mifflin Company, 1989.

Knock at a Star edited by Dorothy M. and X. J. Kennedy. Boston: Little Brown, 1982.

My Tangs Tungled edited by Sara and John Brewton, and G. Meredith Blackburn III. New York: Thomas Y. Crowell Co., 1973.

The Oxford Treasury of Children's Poems edited by Michael Harrison and Christopher Stuart-Clark. Oxford: Oxford University, 1988.

Poetry for Young People, Edgar Allan Poe edited by Brod Bagert. New York: Sterling Publishing Company, 1995. (Includes short explanations of each poem as well as wonderful illustrations that bring the poems to life.)

The Random House Book of Poetry for Children edited by Jack Prelutsky. New York: Random House, 1983.

Red Dragonfly on My Shoulder translated by Sylvia Cassedy and Kunihiro Suetake. USA: HarperCollins Publishers, 1992. (A collection of Haiku poems translated from the Japanese.)

Shrieks at Midnight edited by Sara and John Brewton. New York: Thomas Y. Crowell Co., 1969.

Yours til Banana Splits: 201 Autograph Rhymes edited by Joanna Cole and Stephanie Colmeson. New York: Morrow Jr. Books, 1995.

In addition to his many one-poem books, Jack Prelutsky has also authored several collections of poems. To name a few:
A Pizza the Size of the Sun
Tyrannosaurus Was a Beast
Ride a Purple Pelican
Beneath a Blue Umbrella

Shel Silverstein's collections have been popular with children for many years.
The Giving Tree and *Giraffe and a Half* (1964)
Where the Sidewalk Ends (1974)
The Missing Piece (1976)
A Light in the Attic (1981)
Falling Up: Poems and Drawings (1996)

Myra Cohn Livingston has a series of short collections of her poems which are well worth reading.
Earth Songs
Sky Songs
A Circle of Seasons

Note: There are many books in the poetry section of your library that are devoted to just one poem. These would be ideal for the reading shelf in your classroom. One of my favorites is: *Casey at the Bat* by Ernest Lawrence Thayer. New York: Handprint Books, 2000. The wonderful illustrations by Christopher Bing bring this famous poem to life!

The One Hundred Lines Club

_____

of _____
Student Name

School

has completed every recitation rule.
And therefore is a member of
"The One Hundred Lines Club"!

Congratulations!

_____
Signature

_____
Date

Printed in the USA
CPSIA information can be obtained
at www.ICGtesting.com
LVHW080723170724
785510LV00007B/277

9 781586 830823